EXPLORATIONS
IN ARCHITECTURE

EXPLORATIONS IN ARCHITECTURE

TEACHING
DESIGN
RESEARCH

Issued by the Swiss Federal Office of Culture, Urs Staub
Edited by Reto Geiser

Birkhäuser
Basel · Boston · Berlin

Published in conjunction with the official Swiss contribution
to the 11th International Architecture Exhibition in Venice, 2008.

ISSUED BY the Swiss Federal Office of Culture, *Urs Staub*
EDITED BY *Reto Geiser*

GRAPHIC DESIGN *Philipp Herrmann,*
Ludovic Innocent Varone, Zurich
PHOTOGRAPHY (Inserts and Inside
Cover) *Maris Mezulis*
PRINTING Graphische Anstalt
J. E. Wolfensberger AG, Birmensdorf
BINDING BuBu, Buchbinderei Burkhardt
AG, Mönchaltorf
TYPE Executive Regular
PAPER Munken Print White 115 g/m²,
Alpinacoat 100 g/m² and Truecard 240 g/m²
COPYEDITING *Elizabeth Tucker*, Basel
PROOFREADING *David Koralek*, Berlin
TRANSLATION (from German to English)
Elizabeth Tucker, Basel (*Eisinger, Gramazio &*
Kohler, Josephy, Richter)

Printed on acid-free paper produced
from chlorine-free pulp. TCF ∞

Printed in Switzerland

Selected translations in French, German,
Italian, and Romansh are available at
www.explorationsinarchitecture.ch

Library of Congress Control Number
2 0 0 8 9 3 4 1 5 3

Bibliographic information published by
the German National Library: The German
National Library lists this publication in
the Deutsche Nationalbibliografie. Detailed
bibliographic data are available on the
Internet at http://dnb.d-nb.de.

09.08 2500 860199201

Birkhäuser Verlag AG
Basel · Boston · Berlin
P.O. Box 133, CH-4010 Basel, Switzerland
Part of Springer Science + Business Media

For copyright of illustrations and photographs, see the detailed list in the appendix.
Every reasonable attempt has been made
to identify owners of copyright. Errors or
omissions will be corrected in subsequent
editions.

ISBN: 978–3–7643–8921–5

9 8 7 6 5 4 3 2 1

www.birkhauser.ch

The increasing magnitude and complexity of interacting lives must make us realize that our future depends upon an understanding and control of our common system—a self-regulating, interdependent, dynamic pattern that moves from yesterday into today and from today into tomorrow.
—*Gyorgy Kepes*, Arts of the Environment, *1972*

EXPLORATIONS

ACKNOWLEDGMENTS

This publication is the outcome of a collective effort. Conceiving it and putting it together has been a great pleasure, an intense way of engaging with a fascinating subject matter, and at the same time, a steep race against time. All those involved responded with great excellence, flexibility, and an impressive amount of patience.

Thanks are due to the four research studios—shown in the exhibition at the Swiss Pavilion and presented in this volume—for their efforts toward the completion of this endeavor. Marc Angélil, Dieter Dietz, Fabio Gramazio, Harry Gugger, and Matthias Kohler have all been generous with their work and time. I would like to acknowledge Aline Dubach, Marc Schmitt, and Katia Ritz at ALICE; Henriette Spoerl at LAPA; Michael Knauß, Tobias Bonwetsch, Michael Lyrenmann, Silvan Oesterle, and Nadine Jerchau at DFAB; Jörg Stollmann, Sascha Delz, Lukas Küng, and Dirk Hebel at MAS UD. This book would not exist without the generous contributions of Daniel Bisig, Sanford Kwinter, Bruno Latour, Rolf Pfeifer, Georges Teyssot, and Albena Yaneva. I am indebted to Tom Avermaete, Ole W. Fischer, Kim Förster, Filip Geerts, Andri Gerber, John Harwood, Martin Josephy, Jeannie Kim, Tilo Richter, Deane Simpson, Martino Stierli, and Mark Wasiuta, who all took on the challenging task of compressing their expertise into the highly condensed format of the historical case studies.

I would like to thank Angelus Eisinger, not only for his essay, but also for his unflagging support and all our conversations which have been instrumental in the development of this project. Salomon Frausto has been a critical voice in crucial moments.

Elizabeth Tucker took on the arduous task of copyediting a manuscript of highly varying voices. Tilo Richter generously shared his insights into the production of books and helped to revise the manuscript. I am most grateful to Philipp Herrmann and Ludovic Varone for providing their talent and typographic excellence, and for taking on the impractical task of designing a book without having a final manuscript. Maris Mezulis contributed striking photographs of frequently hidden and unexpected research environments. At Birkhäuser Publishers I would like to thank Nora Kempkens and Andrea Wiegelmann for taking on this project and helping to make it happen.

I am much obliged to Urs Staub at the Swiss Federal Office of Culture for being a generous and intellectually challenging patron, and for his faith in this undertaking. I would like to acknowledge Hans-Rudolf Reust, Andreas Reuter and Isa Stürm for their critical input and support throughout the project.

Collaborating with Fabio Gramazio, Matthias Kohler, and Michael Knauß on the creation of the oscillating wall defining the scenography of the exhibition in the Swiss Pavilion has been a great pleasure and also an invaluable process of learning.

I owe thanks to Christian Keller, CEO of Keller AG Ziegeleien, for his vision and support, to Elisabetta Giordano, who helped me to crunch numbers, to Jerôme Szeemann and Elena Solari, whose patience we stretched beyond limits, and to Serge D'Urach and Atalanta Bouboulis Marcello, without whom our stays in Venice would have been an odyssey.

The exhibition would have not been possible without the contributions of Acomet SA, Alcan Composites, BBZ AG, Fondation Braillard Architectes, Gesellschaft für Technische Zusammenarbeit, Holcim Foundation for Sustainable Construction, IBZ Industrie AG, Keller AG Ziegeleien, KUKA, Maagtechnic, Scobalit AG, Sika Schweiz AG, and Swisspor SA.

The Board of the Swiss Federal Institutes of Technology, the Faculty of Architecture at ETH Zurich, and ENAC, School of Architecture, Civil and Environmental Engineering at EPF Lausanne supported this endeavor significantly. I am especially indebted to Andreas Tönnesmann, Dean of the Faculty of Architecture at ETH Zurich, for his trust and encouragement and for fostering this project while I should have been finalizing my dissertation.

Noëmi Mollet has shared the stresses and exhilarations of this project. I am grateful for her companionship, good spirit, and insight.

—R.G., Basel, July 2008

EXPLORATIONS

INTRODUCTION

Reto Geiser

This volume is not envisioned as a permanent reference—embalming truth for posterity—but as a source that stimulates discourse, questions preconceived notions, searches for new approaches, and expands the open field of architectural research in relation to teaching and design. It is a critical reflection of design methodologies, networks, didactics, and technologies. The goal within these pages is to debate the meaning of "design research" in the applied discipline of architecture, and to provide alternative takes on a term and an academic field that still lack sharp definition. Four exemplars developed at the two Swiss Federal Institutes of Technology at Lausanne and Zurich are contrasted with five critical positions in order to instigate a thought process that will, hopefully, contribute greater clarity. A selection of historical case studies covering seven decades of applied research and didactic experiments in architecture is meant to contextualize these contemporary approaches in the larger disciplinary and cultural context.

It would be presumptuous to claim that design research within the architectural realm is a recent phenomenon. The renaissance of urban investigations and research into digital processes in the 1990s may have partially obscured the fact that a critical investigation and reflection of design methodologies and didactics already existed at the beginning of the previous century. The collaborative research effort, at times even amalgamation, of scientific research with the field of architectural design made a significant leap forward in the mid-twentieth century. With the increased importance of technological research in academics, industry, and the military complex, first interdisciplinary entities such as the RAND Corporation were established. This heightened interest in an international cross-disciplinary and cross-cultural discourse eventually affected the funding of smaller university-based research groups that operated outside of the accustomed sphere, and thus also left a trace in the field of architectural design. New programs were created at many universities, quite frequently blurring the boundaries between science, art, and architecture. One of the first attempts in this direction was an interdisciplinary research project that emerged at the University of Toronto in the 1950s. The Explorations Group—from which the title of this book is adopted— revolving around media guru Marshall McLuhan and anthropologist Edmund Carpenter, also included economists, psychologists, and architects. Research was conducted in collaboration with students and followed a methodology that approached architecture and the urban environment as a framework to analyze the effects of media. Concurrently, new institutions were installed at the Massachusetts Institute of Technology and Harvard University among others, involving such figures as Gyorgy Kepes, Rudolf Arnheim, and Christopher Alexander.

About thirty years ago, Swiss architecture was dominated by practical, construction-oriented concerns as opposed to theoretical or speculative interests. Curricular proposals from the 1970s, prepared by such architects as Paul Hofer and Dolf Schnebli, indicate that the main concern of most architecture schools was the formation of "full-fledged" practitioners, who upon earning their diploma would be ready to build. The tradition of construction has always been a defining characteristic of Swiss architecture. In the building culture of this country, where craft has been embedded in daily life for a long time, and where there continues to be no clear division of labor between design and production, it is still possible for architects to control not only the design, but also the construction of a building from first sketches to its completion. While the field has advanced far beyond a mere preoccupation with the technical fabrication of architecture, it is striking to consider the extent to which the engagement with actual physical contexts and the precision of construction is still ingrained in numerous research and teaching activities—a fact that can be also traced in the work of the four research groups included in this book.

In 1999, at a conference held in Bologna, Italy, twenty-nine European states agreed to an education reform that would change the landscape of European universities. With the Bologna Declaration fully implemented in the fall of 2007, Swiss schools came into compliance with the general aim to harmonize higher education across Europe and the initiative to start

EXPLORATIONS

research activities not only in the humanities and sciences, but also the vast field of design-oriented disciplines. This shift in education policy would have significant consequences for architectural education.

The question that immediately arises in light of these new measures is how research can be defined in a field like architectural design. How can research be grasped semantically in a design-oriented, creative-technical discipline? What is the potential value of treating instruction as an apparatus of research? In the context of architectural design, the otherwise customary distinction between basic and applied research seems unproductive. Architectural research derives its potential not by limiting itself to a concise statement of the problem, but by associating fields of knowledge in a way that does not necessarily adhere to academic convention. Science and the humanities are brought into contact with practice-oriented, heuristic-creative approaches, and thus transform the design process. Design becomes an instrument of research that joins together that which ordinarily remains separate.

Architecture is an inherent part of every society. It is an indicator of political, economic, technological, and cultural conditions, as well as their changes. Our environment is constantly altering, generating new paradoxes, and the role of the architect, too, is subject to continuous reformation. In a time of perceptible technological and socio-economic change, architecture can no longer rely on preconceived concepts, established typologies, and design methodologies—nor can architectural education. Rather than perpetuating a particular formal school, academic style, or pedagogical orthodoxy, institutions need to focus on a critical re-examination of design processes themselves, with an aim to formulating new models of collective learning and research practices.

As the four exemplary research groups indicate—each one devised as a "studio," "laboratory," or "atelier"—individual authorship gives way to a collective group identity. The architecture studio in turn becomes a workshop, a platform for debate, a synthesizer of ideas and concepts, as it takes advantage of the expertise of a wide range of individuals and fields of interest. Architecture is not a self-sufficient discipline. It has always been related to such disciplines as engineering, history, or the arts. Nevertheless, it cannot be the goal to put design research on a level with scientific or scholarly advances. Design research, tied to a heuristic model, grasps the complexity of seemingly irresolvable matter based on

INTRODUCTION *Reto Geiser*

simple rules and a highly selective set of information. The design studio offers a productive environment to conduct research, by engaging in wide-ranging networks, adapting seemingly determined technologies, and testing didactic structures and methodological approaches. The teaching environment operates similarly to a laboratory, where the investigation of projects in parallel sets, examinations based on related models and hypotheses, the evaluation of processes, and a critical debate of the outcome's commonalities and differences all contribute to a smooth transition between research and teaching. The peculiarity of this approach is a radical abbreviation of typical research methodologies; students, typically associated with a studio for not more than a year, operate like "short-term scientists," quickly diving into complex subject matter, extracting suggestive information, always negotiating the delicate balance between ignorance and expertise.

The diverse, open—and maybe even unexpected—series of essays and case studies included here investigates the possible modes of design research and teaching in the field of architecture. This publication thematizes essential points of architectural thought by bringing into focus the conflict and the complexity of spatial, organizational, and production-technical dynamics that characterize any discussion of the discipline. Architecture, almost by definition, is predicated upon experimentation and unwieldy forays into widely divergent inventories of knowledge that challenge and redefine disciplinary boundaries and open up new terrains. Beyond merely presenting the impressive output of the four exemplary research units that comprise the exhibition conceived for the Swiss Pavilion at the 11th Venice Architecture Biennale, this publication offers a widening of perspectives in order to demarcate the possibilities and limitations of this particular manner of exploring the world.

EXPLORATIONS   Historical Case Study

PERFORMATIVE MODERNITIES: REM KOOLHAAS'S
DELIRIOUS NEW YORK AS INDUCTIVE RESEARCH

Deane Simpson

First published in 1978, Rem Koolhaas's *Delirious New York* represented a significant deviation from the dominant strains of architectural discourse at the time. Throughout the 1970s, fervent hostility toward the modernist project provided motivation for a reengagement with architectural history, and an articulation of architecture as a system of communication. This renewed historicism can be viewed as a kind of time-travel that focused on distant—almost exclusively European—periods, and consciously bypassed the more recent decades of twentieth-century modernity, in particular the 1920s, which Henry Russell-Hitchcock had already labeled as a "closed historical epoch." By the end of the 1970s these detours converged in "The Presence of the Past," the First International Exhibition of Architecture in Venice, to which Koolhaas's practice, the Office of Metropolitan Architecture (OMA), was invited to contribute although it was conspicuously out of place. This inaugural biennale presented a reactionary form of what Jürgen Habermas, in his essay "Modernity—An Incomplete Project," would describe as "new historicism." The parallel framing of architecture as a communicative system was influenced by techniques imported from other disciplines, including semiotics and structuralist linguistics. In contrast to these obviously signposted routes, *Delirious New York* turned directly toward the "closed" period of modernity, depicting the architecture of Manhattan not in linguistic or representational terms, but as a kind of performative drive.

Delirious New York sought to deny the closure of modernization through a narrative from its subconscious. In contrast to the self-conscious high modernism of the European tradition, *Delirious New York* represents a "popular" American modernism of Manhattan as its flipside, a modernism of unselfconscious density, the "culture of congestion." The results of the laboratory of Manhattan are less the master-planned products of the architect working as an agent of the state, than an index of modernization's effects on the metropolis itself: "the simultaneous explosion of human density and invasion of new technologies" together with the unregulated forces of capitalism. According to Koolhaas, this undeclared modernism, or "Manhattanism," surpasses that of the European avant-gardes, exceeding both the rationality of Le Corbusier's machine-age modernism and the irrationality of Salvador Dali's paranoid-critical surrealism.

As Cary Siress has suggested, Koolhaas attempts to recuperate an alternative form of modernism through

a "parallactic historiography," in which the object, which has supposedly been exhausted of relevance, is reframed by the point of view assumed by a repositioned subject. Linked to this parallactic view is a conscious rejection of those historiographic tenets that aspire to objective historical truth, a rejection that leads to the blurring of roles which plays out in the book's style and structure. Spanning the registers of journal, screenplay, ethnography, and novel, it reflects Koolhaas's own history prior to studying architecture, both as a journalist and a screenwriter.

Delirious New York operates predominantly in an inductive mode. Induction, which involves the extraction of general principles (theory) from observation of specific phenomena (fact), is typically defined as the obverse of deduction, the application or testing of general principles through the production of specific phenomena. If the modernist manifesto was intended to be read according to a logic of rationalist deduction, then the reversal of this procedure (induction) corresponds to the "retroactive manifesto." In a genetic context, a third term, "transduction," refers to the transfer of coded material from one bacterium to another. In this context, it describes the approach, central to the work of OMA, of transferring Manhattan's genetic code onto the field of their various projects.

This generative mode of polemical architectural "research," directed toward theorizing urban phenomena outside of the architectural profession, had famously been worked through in Robert Venturi, Denise Scott Brown and Steven Izenour's classic *Learning from Las Vegas* (1972), a text that was as influential for Koolhaas as it was for a generation of architects. Koolhaas's "Project on the City" at Harvard University likewise adopted as its primary mode the identification and discussion of other contemporary "Rosetta Stones," a research model that would become commonplace in many schools of architecture. This project has looked to contemporaneously explosive locations of urban growth that are driven by the global market economy, rather than the dictates of architects. Although undeniably productive both in generating lucid interpretations of contemporary urban phenomena and in the acquisition of large building projects, these recent investigations have yet to manifest themselves in OMA's practice with the drive and clarity of *Delirious New York*'s "culture of congestion."

BIBLIOGRAPHY
• Habermas, Jürgen. "Modernity—An Incomplete Project."
In Hal Foster, ed. *The Anti-Aesthetic: Essays on Postmodern Culture*. Seattle, WA: Bay Press, 1983.
• Koolhaas, Rem. *Delirious New York: A Retroactive Manifesto for Manhattan*. New York: Thames and Hudson, 1978.
• Siress, Cary. "The Urban Unconscious: Mediating the Psyche and the City in the Twentieth Century." Dissertation, ETH Zurich, 2005.

REM KOOLHAAS *Deane Simpson*

1   Excerpt from first edition of *Delirious New York*, Arrival of Le Corbusier in New York.
2   Cover from first edition of *Delirious New York*, 1978.
3   Cover from *The Presence of the Past*, catalog to the First International Exhibition of Architecture, Venice Biennale, 1980.
4a   Induction Excerpt from *Delirious New York*, Downtown Athletic Club section, skyscraper as social condenser.
4b   Transduction, excerpt from *Content*, "Universal Modernization Patent," competition scheme for Parc de la Villette, Paris, 1982.

1

Arrival of Le Corbusier in New York. "He looked mollified. . . ."

3

4a   4b

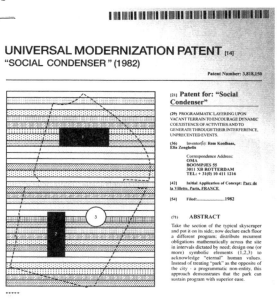

EXPLORATIONS

Essay

STOP MAKING SENSE

Angelus Eisinger

A first thought: maybe design research is just a shimmering landscape of ideas and practices, models and interventions, which extends to the horizon of society and merges into it again and again. This landscape ranges from commentary and analysis, to current spatial realities, to experiments with new materials or production processes. Moments of exploration fuse with moments of reflection in various hybrid relationships. Further, it becomes apparent: this rich and expansive landscape is currently attracting attention far beyond the sphere of architects, a fact that may strike some people as the simultaneity of the non-simultaneous. Differently stated, public interest in the image- and word-constructions of design research is coinciding with a phase in which the opinion seems to be forming that, in the quotidian world of construction and planning, architects now play only a supporting role. Apart from a handful of global stars, the architect today normally only has to decorate what others have already established in terms of content. Assuming that this diagnosis is correct, the internal report on the current situation could scarcely be farther removed from the ambitions that arose at the dawning of modern architecture and accompanied it for quite some time. Across long passages of the twentieth century, the promise for a harmonic development of industrial society was predicated on architects. The architect conceived of him- or herself as the one who would channel the enormous productive forces of industrialization and thus once more would reconcile society and technology, culture and nature. Research served as an important instrument for concretizing the architect's ambitions, as some representative examples of modernist exponents may demonstrate. Consider Walter Gropius and Konrad Wachsmann: their General Panel Plan involved a modular building system for which, through a meticulous conception of the assembly line process, they sought to adjust the industrial logic of production to the requirements of high-quality architecture.

Or, we could cite Ludwig Hilberseimer's attempt to find generally valid planning rules for the systematic composition of urban spaces. We could also take as an example the studies for *Neue Stadt* in Otelfingen: here, painstaking work on the essential components of the modern city reached a pinnacle in an assiduous determination of ideal urban-sociological spatial structures. Finally, this aspect of a "walk on the wild side" of modern standardizing and normalizing attempts is manifest in an exemplary fashion in the works of Ernst Neufert, who was determined to bring nearly every area of human activity in space into the realm of function optimality and to secure them there for all time.

From a distance, it becomes clear that architects have sorely lacked the means, but also the necessary insight into spatial realities, to achieve their goals. If we observe the developments of recent decades, we see that ironically, it is technological and social dynamics that have kept the figure of the architect from attaining the desired central position. However, current technological developments indicate that the influence of technology on architecture cannot be reduced to a simple denominator; rather, this influence points in many directions at once. The digital era is subjecting previous architectural practices and process logics to a fundamental revision, while at the same time new options are presenting themselves for redefining previously problematic interfaces, such as the transition from design to production.

AUTO-DIAGNOSES

Several years ago, faced with this kaleidoscope of inherited self-conceptions, reformulated claims and stubborn context determinants, Rem Koolhaas spoke of architecture as a "fuzzy amalgamation of ancient knowledge and contemporary practice." He went on to say that in its modest success at determining reality, architecture seems an "awkward way to look at the world and an inadequate medium to operate on it." In other words, as a building practice, architecture visibly lacks the power of influence to determine the course of things in space. Robbed of its empirical significance, it derives its legitimacy through making current its rich cultural tradition, which for Koolhaas presents itself as a singular "way of thinking about anything" and as a "diagram of everything."[1]

[1]   Rem Koolhaas and Brendan McGetrick, eds., *Content* (Cologne: Taschen, 2004), 6.

EXPLORATIONS

Essay

If we follow these auguries, then architecture manifests itself as an instrument for exploring the world. We could also say being research is one of the constitutive properties of architecture. Particularly in these times of persistent confusion, architecture as research offers the option to preserve a view of the total. In this way it emerges, next to science and art, as a third form of penetrating the world. Design research operates according to its own principles, conventions, and ways of reading. It is distinct from the two other approaches to the world in that it keeps itself apart both from scientific conventions of methodologically secured gains in knowledge, and from the radical subjectivity of art. So if architecture in fact comprises this distinct approach to the world, how can design research be described?

THE SOCIAL SHADOWS CAST ON ARCHITECTURE
The transitions between architecture and design research are fluid.[II] Therefore, in order to inquire into design research, it is necessary to be clear about what architects actually do. The answer seems trivial: architects design and build, and images, sketches, plans, models and texts are their means of articulating and communicating their ideas. Here, architecture appears as an offer being made to society; the contents of this offer are either perceived or not.

As plausible as this approach might initially sound, it in fact belies all essential facets of the relationship between architecture and society, as any practicing architect would readily confirm. So how can these influential relationships be characterized?

The conception of the interdependence of science and society that Bruno Latour developed in his actor-network theory can also cast some light on the interweaving of architecture and its social context.[III] Following Latour, I would like to propose understanding architecture as a sequence of translation and back-translation processes from society into architecture and from architecture into society. What does this perspective say about encounters between the two? For one thing, it is striking that in all of its representations, architecture locates itself in the midst of the events of society. Thus, the "diagram of everything" that characterizes architecture according to Koolhaas can also be understood in the most literal sense: in architecture, society becomes visible in all its complexity—but not as a direct mirroring of social relationships. The social presence in architecture is only revealed to us in its entire scope when we develop a sharper view of

STOP MAKING SENSE *Angelus Eisinger*

the innumerable encounters in which the social context and architecture come into contact and exert their influence on one another.

It is advisable to make simplifying distinctions between design, realization, and use of an architectural object.[IV] In each of these phases, society realizes itself in architecture in a specific way. Design represents a microcosm, a model of the world that explicitly and implicitly reflects, addresses and formulates society in space and in its materiality. In the phase of realization, this model is implemented: one could also say it is given a reality check. In this phase, the many demands that the design consciously or unconsciously imposes on the social context become visible as behaving in a certain way. These demands can appear in the form of construction methods, market conditions or assumptions about political constellations. If they cannot be realized, the design must correspondingly be adjusted — in some cases beyond recognition. Thus, implementation deforms the intentions of a design. Finally, we come to the last of our ideally typical phases, that of appropriation and use. In this phase, it becomes evident to what extent the expectations and promises that design once formulated for everyday spatial life will hold true. It is in the course of their behavior that residents and users articulate their accordance to the designer's propositions. Design research relates to the social context in a way that is similar to architecture. If design research is operating *as* design, then design research also inscribes its demands on the social context. As the research of built or urban constellations, it encounters at every turn the social fabric that architecture is woven into. So if we understand research as a process of discovery, what does design research reveal?

A BRIEF OUTLINE OF FOUR DESIGN RESEARCH LABORATORIES
The Swiss Pavilion at this year's Architecture Biennale surveys and explores the open field of design research by presenting the works of four design studios at the Swiss Federal Institutes of Technology in Lausanne and Zurich.

II   Compare Sanford Kwinter's article "Soft Systems" on architecture as a 'soft science,' in *Culture Lab 1*, ed. Brian Boigon (New York: Princeton Architectural Press, 1993), 207–236.

III   In particular the following volumes by Bruno Latour should be mentioned: *Science in Action: How to Follow Scientists and Engineers through Society* (Cambridge: Harvard University Press, 1987); *The Pasteurization of France*, trans. Alan Sheridan and John Law (Cambridge: Harvard University Press, 1988); *Pandora's Hope: Essays on the Reality of Science Studies* (Cambridge: Harvard University Press, 1999).

IV   Also compare Angelus Eisinger and Stefan Kurath, "The Emerging Role of Architects," *Graz Architecture Magazine 4* (2008); Angelus Eisinger, *Städte bauen. Stadtentwicklung und Städtebau in der Schweiz 1940–1970* (Zurich: gta Verlag, 2004).

EXPLORATIONS

Essay

Each studio embodies a distinct conception of research in architecture. Different priorities, perspectives and motivations become evident, as briefly outlined here.

The LAPA of Harry Gugger in Lausanne concerns itself with the determiners and options of architectural work on the basis of concrete urban situations, such as a neighborhood in Havana. In the process, it integrates all levels of scale, from the building site of a targeted intervention to reflections on the entire city. At the same time, the laboratory incorporates all phases of architectural work, from development of a comprehensive understanding of urban everyday life to design and hypothetical implementation in construction. Research thus consists of the integration of systematically acquired knowledge into design and its concretization in building.

The ALICE laboratory of Dieter Dietz and his group situates itself in the field of interactions between digital and analog manifestations of architectural design. The group focuses on the moment of learning as a consequence of making. The repeated confrontation of the generated models with alternative conceptions of space expands architectural expressivity in time, as well as making architecture address its own context.

The MAS Urban Transformation in Developing Territories, under the direction of Marc Angélil, has in recent years been engaged in various ways with the everyday urban life of Addis Ababa. Beginning with a heuristic understanding of urban development as "forms of negotiation," the project exposes in various iterations the local production processes of urban spatial realities. Thus, on the one hand a foundation is laid for design interventions that possess the necessary sensitivity to the otherness of this reality. On the other hand, insights gained on location condense into an understanding of the contextual contingencies of planning, which extend far beyond the concrete area under examination.

Finally, the studio of Fabio Gramazio and Matthias Kohler examines through its manipulations of robots the relationship between digital technologies, architecture and production. Designs are generated that can no longer be implemented with traditional fabrication processes, but can only be built by correspondingly programmed robots. Thus, the computer brings design and building closer together and anchors both technology and production in the architect's immediate sphere of influence.

STOP MAKING SENSE *Angelus Eisinger*

SEVEN MARKERS OF DESIGN RESEARCH

From the interviews with the directors of the four architecture studios and in the output of their studio work, design research emerges as a multi-layered mesh of disciplinary self-conceptions and patterns of discourse, thematic foci and methodological approaches. Such a formation cannot be measured absolutely according to the theory of science, nor can it be reduced to a few basic principles without losing its empirical richness. Thus, we should approach the fact of "design research" as cautiously as archaeologists approach their sites of excavation. We will now position seven markers, one by one, in order to survey the diverse thematic terrain that comprises design research in action, as well as its significance.[V]

Amid all the dissimilarities and idiosyncrasies of the four different design research approaches represented here, these markers allow a differentiated, clearly contoured field of epistemologies, working modalities and forms of materialization.

A BRIEF ENCOUNTER

The promises of the moment form the narrative basis of David Lean's melo-dramatic film *Brief Encounter.* On a certain day, two people's paths cross. Thus a love story begins that offers to each person's reality new spaces of possibility far beyond what everyday life is even capable of recognizing. In Lean's film, the subversive productivity of the coincidental ends in catastrophe. What first appears as a plausible option wrecks itself on conventions and the implacability of the social context. In the plot of *Brief Encounters,* metaphorical relations to design research can be gleaned. In architecture, bodies of knowledge from different disciplines often encounter each other only fleetingly and partially, and nevertheless come into contact in a shower of sparks. In such moments it becomes evident that architecture, in contrast to the social- and even more to the natural sciences, is not caught up in the "truth of the discipline" and consequently does not have to abide by the conditions that Michel Foucault determined as prerequisites to modern scientific thought and work.[VI] Out of the momentary incompleteness of brief encounters with other disciplines, a distinct creativity is generated in

V   "In action" makes clear the focus of this approach to design research via the concrete processes through which this research is carried out. The phrase is borrowed from the title of Bruno Latour's essential study from 1987, *Science in Action:* *How to Follow Scientists and Engineers through Society.*

VI   Michel Foucault, *Die Ordnung des Diskurses* [1970], trans. Walter Seitter (Frankfurt am Main: Fischer Taschenbuch Verlag, 1991), 24.

EXPLORATIONS

Essay

architecture and design research. The relationships between the disciplines are products of the situation and of the intellectual agility of the participants. This form of interdisciplinarity is focused and it secures the transitions to other disciplines only as is deemed necessary in the moment. Contradictions and irreconcilabilities between different disciplinary axioms and ways of thinking and working become less influential and a space emerges for associative thinking, which generates innovations precisely because it ignores complexities or approaches them intuitively. Herein lies the extraordinary productivity of architecture's wild thinking, which knows almost no taboos. As in Lean's melodrama, however, the context poses a constant threat, since associations offer the temptation to negate context conditions and to make many-layered contingent realities manageable in overly simple models. In this way, architecture curtails its own possible options.

THE WHOLE AND NOT THE PARTS
Since the industrial revolution, the whole has been the constitutive domain of architecture. The operations of CIAM, its work within a comprehensive but integrated system of levels of scale, stand for insight into the necessity of advancing into the total. This conceptual logic has an empirical counterpart. For example, Manfredo Tafuri's examinations on the development of urbanist discussion and production during the Weimar Republic showed how the implementation of the modern counter model in the capitalistically determined metropolis required a stable framework of many different interests.[VII] From financing, to land laws, to progress in rationalization in the building sector, to political support, all interests had to be committed to this goal. It is not surprising that constellations so dense with prerequisites could only be established in a few cases—in particular in Frankfurt am Main under Ernst May, but there, too, only for a short time, between 1925 and 1930.

This characteristic of the examined design research studios—i.e. the renewed responsibility of architecture for all levels of the scale—calls for a culture of the whole. The whole surmounts specialization. This demand appears in the four studios' design research in two different possible guises. First, as with Gramazio and Kohler, the research setting can reduce the complexity of reality as much as possible. Observation and organization of production processes allow the initial conditions for successful design research to be ascertained, designated and manipulated.

STOP MAKING SENSE   *Angelus Eisinger*

The second possibility consists in capturing the whole *in* design research. Here, too, there remains a residual difference between master and copy. This difference determines the extent to which empirically productive insights about the conditions and possibilities of architectural activities can be generated at all.

CONFIDENCE AND RECENTERING

Maybe design research only states with exceptional frankness the intention that research always pursues, i.e. to gain control over the context. The four studios are also conducted so as to overcome the precarious position of the architect and to strengthen the architect's role in the daily world of construction and planning.

The fields of research thus serve to recapture a lost social position. Design research provides empirically validated insights necessary for that purpose. The synoptic ability is no longer grounded in a genius omniscience that still fascinated modernists, but in "confidence and not ability," as Harry Gugger stated in his interview. In other words, the exhaustion of the grand narratives of modernism also eliminated the integrating center. The architect after modernism is now readying him- or herself via research to clarify the architect's role in the production process of the individual object and of urban spaces, and thus to regain control of the lost center. Design research informs him or her about strategically indispensible alliances and tactical options. Thus, as the division of labor advances, it turns a threat to the professional field into the motivation to take on coordination.

DESIGN PROCESSES AS PROCESSES OF RESEARCH

Designing is not only the condensation of knowledge and skills into a structure. Designing as a process is also an autonomous form of knowledge production. This knowledge cannot be made to conform with the usual categories of measurement. Design is daring to look ahead. It constantly stirs up the genteel and tidy orderings of conventional research work. What afterwards emerges as knowledge cannot be anticipated, but it can be fed back into the daily task of research.

VII   Manfredo Tafuri, *The Sphere and the Laby-rinth: Avant-Gardes and Architecture from Piranesi* *to the 1970s*, trans. Pellegrino d'Acierno et al. (Cambridge, MA: MIT Press, 1987).

EXPLORATIONS

Essay

TACIT KNOWLEDGE AND MEDIA OF COMMUNICATION
The physician and philosopher Michael Polyani used the term "tacit knowledge" to denote knowledge that people bring to a situation and unconsciously activate as needed.[VIII] This knowledge is difficult to communicate
or to codify. With the dictum "we know more that we can tell," Polyani
referred to certainties acquired through practice, without which it would
not be possible to conduct research. Architecture works by connecting
media. Text, image and model are joined into complex statements about space
and its properties. Digital media have given rise to fundamental transformations, from the generation of ideas to building production: the realism of
the renderings goes far beyond the possibilities of previous representation
techniques. Computer-based programs compose once unthinkable structural
models and CAM brings design and production closer together via the
computer. Meanwhile, tacit knowledge gives architects the necessary basis
to connect these dynamics plausibly. It enables complex situations to be
quickly decoded and made manageable, including self-evident skills such as
the interpretation of particular phenomena and the agility to associate the
contents of various media. Through tacit knowledge, the interrelationships
between digital and physical/analog media of articulation can be productively
applied, as in the case of Dieter Dietz's ALICE. In this way, catalytic
processes of design emerge. Research is carried out as a learning through
making that decodes the messages of media and feeds these back into
the design process. Thus, tacit knowledge allows technologies to be instru-
mentalized and assembled.

PHYSICAL REALITY
Since its beginnings, architecture has always been an art of fabrication.
It has come to know worlds of self-referential reflection and cognition, and
to inhabit these through designs and theoretical discourses that are absolved
of the necessity of proof in reality. But as long as architecture aspires towards physical reality, these will remain secondary spheres, though inspiring
ones.
　　　In the four cases presented here, design research also aspires for
the metamorphosis in material of what is thought and conceived. In the
interview with Gramazio and Kohler it is made explicit: "Design research is
changing physical reality." The research tests setups and sequences, and
feeds the resulting knowledge into its own ongoing course. What's more,

STOP MAKING SENSE   *Angelus Eisinger*

as these processes are reconstructed, procedures and constellations become evident that constitute architecture as a practice. Making building a reference point of research also means illuminating those elements that secure the influence of architecture. Actor-network theory speaks of "immutable mobiles," technologically stabilized alliances between actor and artifact that solve problems in a particular way independently of their context. Immutable mobiles manifest the success of research and development. As already discussed, architectural modernism exhausted itself in making such immutable facts. Current design research no longer chases after formulas, universal types or building components that would be capable of solving a particular problem once and for all. Instead, it seeks within constellations the invariants that permit stable networks between the figure of the architect and the involved actors and determinants. Thus the attempt is no longer to fix elements and characteristics, but rather their processes.

SUBJECTIVITY / OBJECTIVITY

The fascination for the achievements and the methodological consistency of the engineering sciences has accompanied architecture for a long time. Across the twentieth century, reproducibility was the standard by which the compatibility of artistic architectural creation and industrial logic had to prove itself. In this way, architecture's productive subjectivity would turn itself into objectivity.

In his history of modern architecture, the equally attentive and empathetic observer Leonardo Benevolo diagnosed the situation in the year 1970, with a certain discomfort, as the fragmentation of this tradition of research into multiple, concurrent instances of "subjective, tendentious architecture research."[IX] Benevolo formulated his critique at a time when the banal, industrially produced masses of houses, buildings and neighborhoods seemed to allow no outlet from the cul-de-sac into which the reproduction ideal had fallen.

Today, we can see that Benevolo's lamented loss of unity in method and inquiry was directly followed in recent years by an astonishing productivity in design research—accompanied by an uncommon attention to media. The flood of publications in which architects confront the realities of the

VIII   Michael Polanyi, *The Tacit Dimension* (London: Routledge & Kegan Paul, 1967), especially chapter 1.

IX   Leonardo Benevolo, *Geschichte der Architektur des 19. und 20. Jahrhunderts*, vol. III (Munich: DTV, 1988), 74.

EXPLORATIONS

Essay

world with their perspectives shows no sign of letting up. This newest generation of design research does not lament the lack of a common theoretical foundation. Design research no longer aspires to resolve its observations and conclusions into the general. Instead, it presents itself as reflections, interpretations and diagnoses, which repeatedly subject the whole to commentary and analysis. Architecture today noticeably refrains from a decision in the old debate as to whether it is an art or a science, and thus keeps all of its methodological options open. What in early modernism was highly sought after, the stringency of clearly outlined, building- and planning-directed research questions that supposedly culminate in objectivity and optimization, yields knowledge with a consciously limited scope. These insights, however, do not accumulate into a continually expanding body of knowledge that could be ordered and developed according to the conventions of a discipline; they possess only brief half-lives. The results of current design research resemble offered interpretations; the power of these interpretations to influence further development only arises along the convoluted paths of a reception that cannot be controlled.

LIMITATION OF SENSE IS THE BEGINNING OF MORE SENSE
Scattered across the expansive field of design research in action, it is now possible to locate seven markers. How are they arranged, and what do they say about design research? To begin with, it is remarkable in the four Swiss examples how strongly academic work and thinking in this country continues to focus on the processes of concrete building and planning. This focus, and the treatment of these empirical dynamics, demonstrates the exceptional position that Swiss architecture occupies in the current situation. At the same time, the markers make it possible to recognize particularities of design research that come into play well beyond the Swiss context. Design research today operates in a way that is thematically situative and also behaves agilely in questions of method. Such research does not aspire to reveal every last secret. It conducts an economy of sense production that pursues exploration of the world only to the extent that the results contribute to architecture. The customary scientific-theoretical division into basic and applied research has defeated itself. Its vanishing points of the essence of things or of optimization are no longer of interest. The empirically true is also not the business of design research. Thus, design research does not scrupulously trace the social reality of archi-

STOP MAKING SENSE *Angelus Eisinger*

tecture. Instead, design research proceeds according to the maxim "stop making sense." It knows that only through limiting the field of vision can the total come into view.

SELECTED MILESTONES IN SWISS DESIGN RESEARCH
- Martin, Camille, and Hans Bernoulli. *Städtebau in der Schweiz: Grundlagen*. Ed. by Bund Schweizer Architekten. Zurich: Verlag Fretz & Wasmuth, 1929.
- Meili, Armin, ed. *Bauliche Sanierung von Hotels und Kurorten. Schlussbericht*. Erlenbach: Verlag für Architektur, 1945.
- Carol, Hans, and Max Werner, eds. *Städte – wie wir sie wünschen. Ein Vorschlag zur Gestaltung schweizerischer Grossstadt-Gebiete, dargestellt am Beispiel von Stadt und Kanton Zürich*. Zurich: Regio-Verlag, 1949.
- Egli, Ernst, et. al. *Die Neue Stadt. Eine Studie für das Furttal*. Zurich: Verlag Bauen + Wohnen, 1961.
- Oswald, Franz, and Peter Baccini. *Netzstadt: Designing the Urban*. In cooperation with Mark Michaeli. Basel / Boston / Berlin: Birkhäuser Verlag, 2003.
- Diener Roger, Jacques Herzog, Marcel Meili, et. al. *Switzerland: An Urban Portrait*. Basel / Boston / Berlin: Birkhäuser Verlag, 2006.

EXPLORATIONS   Historical Case Study

ALTERNATIVE EDUCATIONAL PROGRAMS IN ARCHITECTURE: THE INSTITUTE FOR ARCHITECTURE AND URBAN STUDIES

Kim Förster

The Institute for Architecture and Urban Studies is known for its publications, especially *Oppositions* and *Skyline*. Nevertheless, it was originally conceived as an alternative to established schools of architecture. Founded by Peter Eisenman with the support of the trustees of the Museum of Modern Art and Cornell University, when it began operations in Midtown Manhattan in the fall of 1967, it presented itself as an "independent educational corporation" whose declared goal was to enhance the system of architectural education as well as planning processes. By acquiring public contracts, it intended to bridge "the gap between the theoretical world of the university and the pragmatic world of the planning agencies," and to achieve social relevance for architecture.

Graduate students were invited to attend an urban design studio and work on concrete urban projects. The entire range of physical planning was integrated, from conceptual design to implementation. In addition, the faculty offered seminars in the theory of architecture and urban design, as well as in the social sciences, humanities, and engineering. In the initial period, the Institute was heavily dependent on tuition, and the relationship to MoMA's Department of Architecture under Arthur Drexler was crucial both financially and on the level of ideas. Research was exhibited in close cooperation between the two organizations. The jointly organized conferences "Architecture Education U.S.A." and "Universitas Project" both made substantial contributions to the debate on architectural education.

By the time the AIA honored the Institute for its research and educational programs in 1976, a reorientation had already taken place. New York's financial crisis had resulted in a shortage of publicly financed projects, and so the Institute was no longer conceived of as a research institution. Instead, with an extension of the network of fellows, staff, and guests, it was systematically transformed into a teaching center and claimed three new territories: the architectural journal *Oppositions,* which was promoted as an instrument of dialogue with architects, theoreticians and historians overseas, especially in Italy; an exhibitions program, which would go on to host thirty-two shows altogether; and an evening lecture series directed not only to architects, but also to a lay audience. Educational programs were added for undergraduate students from colleges that did not have schools of architecture, and for high school students to learn basic architectural principles.

In the second half of the 1970s, the Institute developed into a public forum for the debate on architecture in New York City. In the spring of 1977 an interdisciplinary series of lectures was organized. "City as Theater" drew from Lewis Mumford's *Culture of Cities* in considering the city as both a physical frame and a dramatic setting. Experts from different disciplines and professions lectured about the drama of life in New York City. Admission to the eighteen evening lectures was free.

With generous support from the National Endowment for the Humanities, in 1977 the Institute started what would be its biggest project in architectural education, OPEN PLAN. In the four associated lecture series, Architecture, The City, The Arts, and Design, architecture was discussed as an expression of American culture. For three academic years, lectures and follow-up seminars were offered each night of the week, and every four weeks a unique, open round table discussion between the disciplines was hosted. This program was the final step in institutionalizing a culture of debate in architectural and urbanistic circles in New York City. It is within this framework that Rem Koolhaas, who had been a visiting fellow at the Institute before, presented *Delirious New York* in the autumn of 1978, just in time for the publication of his first monograph.

An Advanced Design Workshop was installed in 1978, which ought to have profited from the intellectual ambition of the seminars of OPEN PLAN. Next to other respectable architects, the Institute managed to acquire Aldo Rossi, who also was lecturing at Yale at that time. When Peter Eisenman resigned as Director in 1982, his successor saw his main task as simply to maintain the status quo until the Institute was shut down in 1984. Ultimately, it seems that its historical relevance is not derived from the didactics, methods and contents of its educational programs. Rather, the Institute was able to play to the gallery by identifying a target audience that reached from ninth grade to postdoctoral students and beyond. On this basis it installed a complex, far-reaching network of architectural educators, which has decisively marked US architectural culture and which is still active today.

BIBLIOGRAPHY
• Ambasz, Emilio, ed. *The Universitas Project. Solutions for a Post-Technological Society.* New York: The Museum of Modern Art, 2006. Reader documenting 1972 conference.
• Goldberger, Paul. "Midtown Architecture Institute Flowering as a Students Mecca." In *New York Times*, 30 October 1975, 41, 77.
• Sorkin, Michael. "Reforming the Institute." In *Village Voice.* 30 April 1985. Reprinted in Sorkin, Michael. *Exquisite Corpse. Writing on Buildings.* London/New York: Verso, 1991, 109–113.
• "The Institute for Architecture and Urban Studies," *Casabella* 359/360, December 1971, 100–102.

INSTITUTE FOR ARCHITECTURE AND URBAN STUDIES *Kim Förster*

1   Poster designed by Massimo
Vignelli for the lecture series "City as
Theater," held at the Institute for Archi-
tecture and Urban Studies between
March 1 and June 29, 1977

1

THE INSTITUTE FOR ARCHITECTURE AND URBAN STUDIES
8 WEST 40th STREET, NEW YORK, NEW YORK 10018

EVENING PROGRAM IN ARCHITECTURE AND PLANNING

CITY AS THEATER

18 free public forums open to all those interested in the drama of life in New York City. Tuesdays, 7:30 PM at The Institute for Architecture and Urban Studies, 8 West 40th Street, New York, New York. These events are made possible with support from the New York Council for the Humanities. For further information contact Mimi Shanley at 212-398-9474.
"The city in its complete sense then, is a geographic plexus, an economic organization, an institutional process, a theater of social action, and an esthetic symbol of collective unity. On one hand it is a physical frame for the commonplace domestic and economic activities; on the other, it is a consciously dramatic setting for the more sublimated urges of a human culture. The city fosters art and *is* art; the city creates the theater and *is* the theater. It is in the city, the city as theater that man's more purposive activities are formulated and worked out through conflicting and cooperating personalities, events, groups, into more significant culminations." Lewis Mumford, *The Culture of Cities.*

PART I: BETWEEN UTOPIA AND THE EVERYDAY
ERIKA MUNK, MODERATOR

March 1
Michael Bristol, Critic
Utopia: Procession, Charivari and Riot.
Conflict and Utopian Horizons.
Mary Henderson, Historian
The Everyday: A History of the Theater as City
and The Future of the City as Theater

March 8
Donald M. Kaplan, Psychoanalyst
The Psyche: Social Anxiety, Shyness and Stagefright
Max Kozloff, Historian
The Eye: Posing and Peering:
The Voyeuristic Eye on New York

March 15
William Gass, Philosopher
Inside: External Stimulation and Internal Contemplation:
True Drama, External Events and the Atmosphere of Paris
Irving Lavin, Historian
Outside: The Relationship Between the Baroque Stage
and the Baroque Piazza
Roberto Brambilla, Architect
In-Between: Pedestrian Drama in Contemporary Public Spaces

March 22
Brooks McNamara, Professor of Drama
Performance: Theatrical Notions Applied to Spatial
Configurations in the Found Environment
Marilyn Wood, Dancer
Ritual: Reinventing Public Festival and Community
Celebration in the Built Environment

March 29
Richard Gilman, Professor
Audience: The Urban Audience and the Rural Theater
Richard Foreman, Director
Spectator: The Non-Public Play
John Rockwell, Historian
Listener: Experimental Opera in Berlin in the 1920's:
The Provinces and the Capital of the Weimar Republic

PART II: BETWEEN REHEARSAL AND PERFORMANCE
JOHN ROCKWELL, MODERATOR

April 5
Barry Ulanov, Historian
Drama: The Theater of the City.
Dramatic Theory for Architectural Performance
Wendy Perron, Critic
Choreography: Buildings and Dancers,
Inside and Out
Carl Schorske, Historian
Promenade: Wagner and Semper
From the Viennese Opera to the Public Square

April 12
Robert Christgau, Critic
The Crowd: Mass Society, Popular Culture and Rock-n-roll:
Newport, Woodstock and Altamont
Thomas Johnson, Critic
Intermission: Popular Entertainment and
the American Sport
Austin Pendleton, Actor
Rehearsal: The Proscenium Arch and Ideas
About Practice

April 19
Alan Nagler, Historian
The Profane: Mediaeval Street Theater:
When the City Became Theater
Candy Pratts, Designer
The Profane: Bloomingdale's Vignettes:
Reflections of Everyday Life
John Rockwell, Historian
The Profane: Mediaeval vs. Contemporary
Dionysian Rites

April 26
Richard Sennett, Sociologist
Clothing: Street Dress as a Barometer of Public Health
Stella Blum, Historian
Costume: Fashion as a Mirror of Culture

PART III: BETWEEN FANTASY AND REALITY
JOAN DAVIDSON, MODERATOR

May 3
Walter Karp, Author
Reality: The Meaning of the Public Realm:
Public Life, Social Life and Private Life
August Heckscher, Author
Reality: Outdoor Spaces for Acting Out Utopia
Edgar Gregersen, Anthropologist
Fantasy: Latin Music, Puerto Rican Bars and
Social Condensers

May 10
Rosalind Krauss, Historian
The Bacchanalian: Bloomingdale's as Theater of
Consumption
Lee Baxandall, Editor
The Dionysian: Nudes Ascending the Escalators
Eileen Shields, Journalist
Bloomingdale's: Private Enterprise as Public Market

May 17
Lee Breuer, Professor
Indiana: Zuni Theater Life vs. New York Theater Life
Ming Cho Lee, Designer
Lights: Stagesets as Urban Images
William Bonifacio and Catherine Wolfman
Action: The Making of New York Bus Stop Shelters

May 24
Reyner Banham, Historian
Visions: The City as Power and Light.
Starting From Times Square
Gloria Levitas, Anthropologist
Notions: Issues of Participation
Richard Stone, Historian
Projections: Commerce, Utopia and Mass Carnival
at Coney Island

May 31
Martin Pawley, Architect
Private: The Disintegration of the Public Realm:
Newspapers, Television and American Life
Charlayne Hunter-Gault
Public: The Rhythm of the Harlem Drug Market
on the New York Street

PART IV: BETWEEN SPACE AND PLACE
PAUL GOLDBERGER, MODERATOR

June 7
Karl Linn, Psychologist
The Natural: Green Theater
Elizabeth Hardwick, Critic
The Unnatural: City Outside, Horrors Inside
Charles Young, Activist
The Fabricated: Doing Theater to Save the City:
Rat Relocation vs. the Dallas Landlords
The Green Gorillas, Urban Farmers
Underground: Planting New York

June 14
Peter Brooks, Professor of Literature
Word: The Text of the City.
Balzac, Baudelaire and Paris in the 19th Century
Neil Harris, Sociologist
Place: Visual History of Lobbies as Places to Wait

June 21
Anson Strauss, Anthropologist
Image: The Public Fabric and American Urban Imagery
Jason Epstein, Publisher
Symbol: The World Trade Center:
Drama Between the Sky and the Ground
William H. Whyte, Observer
Traffic: Choreography of Plazas and Streets

June 29
Richard Wade, Historian
Civic: The Public Fabric and Policies for
Preserving Public Works
Nicolas Faure, Photographer
Public: Comedy of Manners
Harold Prodansky, Psychologist
Comment: Good Noise, Bad Noise
Doris Freedman, Planner
Response: Making Private Art for Public Places
Louise Kruger, Sculptor
Public Art: A Lion in the Street
John Lindsay, Lawyer
Comment

A

A

METHODOLOGY

METHODOLOGY

Essay

A DISCOURSE ON METHOD
(For the Proper Conduct of Reason and the Search for Efficacity in Design)

Sanford Kwinter

Among the most important questions posited in the twentieth century—
and one whose sheer audacity and hubris was ridiculed long before it was
applauded or seriously taken up—was the question "What is Life?"
      Legend has it that the physicist Erwin Schrödinger was the first to
formulate the question (in his book of the same title of 1944), though we
should recognize that his book was really only the first time a *physicist* had
posited the problem in full seriousness, thereby lending to the query the
gravity and respectability that the nascent field of biology was at that time
still incapable of. Schrödinger's work was, of course, in the field of quantum
mechanics—his popular fame is frequently tied to his parable/paradox
known as "Schrödinger's cat," a curious animal that is both dead and alive
at the same time but that can appear in only one or the other of these
states to a single moment's observation. In those days, quantum mechanics
was a field of developing understanding, increasingly riven with paradoxes
and conundrums, a great many of which have never been unraveled.
Matter was increasingly being known to do some very strange things, and
becoming alive, self-motivating and active was for the first time hypothesized to be one of them.
      It is important to note that biologists, physiologists and naturalists,
not to mention poets, philosophers and mathematicians, had been asking
the same question for a long time and positing some very rich concepts and
theories in response. The European Romantic movement in fact, from Goethe
and Diderot to Coleridge to Thomas Mann, was centrally obsessed with the
question and thought very deeply indeed about the problem of life. In many
ways their reflections were more subtle and fruitful than Schrödinger's.
The principle difference is that the Romantic thinkers saw "life" as a broad,
even general, problem of large scale and large ensembles; they saw it in

A

1a 1b

its macroscopic physical context, and in its relationship to a general quickening and excitation of matter. They saw life as a phenomenon, not of parts and processes added together, but of miraculous wholes.

The problem of wholes has dogged the life sciences, and since the Second World War, the physical sciences as well. If we look at Schrödinger's book, we see two or three fundamental breakthroughs—useful, but no more than that—and then a fourth, one so bizarre as to have been at the time routinely dismissed, but which today seems strangely attractive. The first breakthrough was in his coining a phrase based on thermodynamics and thinking of it in terms of information flow and not purely of energy. That term was "negative entropy." Life was seen as a problem of maintaining order over time. The second breakthrough was in positing the idea that the microscopic structure of matter—its actual geometry—might somehow provide the conditions for the active management of ongoing productive processes. He spoke about "aperiodic solids," or solids that do not exhibit formal symmetry. Life was a process that necessarily unfolded from an asymmetrical matrix. The third breakthrough was in his hypothesis that life might well be the product of activities whose instructions are lodged in a code that can be unfolded and read out from microscopic molecular geometries or arrangements. Aperiodic solids, unlike periodic—or regular—ones, have a low level of redundancy in their structures: in principle, they can carry a great deal of information. Life could well be a process whose developmental impetus is stored in a code; in fact not only stored but *read out*.

This was all very hypothetical at the time, but within a decade the solving of the double helix structure of DNA, made possible by Rosie Franklin and X-ray crystallography—an early form of modeling and picturing shapes otherwise unavailable to human senses, but not to intuitions—showed that Schrödinger's speculations were largely true.

At the close of the book, the fourth breakthrough—unorthodox as it may seem—is Schrödinger's Hinduism-inspired speculation that complex

figs. 1a,b

METHODOLOGY

Essay

forms and patterns—for example human consciousnesses—might well be holographic embeddings within larger, more pervasive pattern-forms such as the form of a unitary "universal consciousness," a vibrating medium that connects other differentiated, vibrating bodies.

Aside from Schrödinger's final, incomplete and unsubstantiated fourth hypothesis, all the other concepts belonged to a template theory of life as a pattern to be somehow miraculously copied and set in motion. On the other hand, the Romantic writers and philosophers, and the life scientists at the end of the nineteenth century, were largely preoccupied with life as a global phenomenon, a global form whose principle feature was its capacity to integrate. They were preoccupied with life as a derivative of wholeness.

Yet Schrödinger's Hinduism had really very powerfully imprinted his thinking. His thoughts about life as a phenomenon requiring special explanation led to the famous formulation in which he compares the repeating pattern of a wallpaper motif whose module may be well-dissimulated by a strategy of staggered tiling, but which in the end adds up to nothing but this: a selfsame module repeated at regular alternating intervals.

Life however, he explained, is a pattern of a different type. Life is a pattern, like the ones we find in tapestries, in which the motif is unitary, total, integrated, essentially partless, unique in all its aspects, hierarchical, and whole. You simply cannot break it down; nor can you build it up. It is given all at once and all of it counts. The order is embedded.

Now if we look at his famous "wave function collapse" in which a unit of matter presents simultaneously as a wave and as a particle right up to the moment that it is formally observed, we notice the same formulation taking place: the particle is literally "smeared" across space so that it can be virtually located everywhere simultaneously within a field, but once fig. 2   pinpointed, it loses its cloudlike omni-locatability. It is no longer everywhere, but only right here (where you chose to measure it).

It was Paul Dirac who invented the concept of "superposition"—according to which a piece of matter such as an electron can exist simultaneously as a particle and a wave—but Schrödinger used it to show how matter existed in space. The relationship of the distributed wave to the locatable particle—the selfsame thing in two different states—seems to have been his model both for consciousness and for life. The relationship is one of superposition and embeddedness. Of course Schrödinger did not go this far. His reflections on life seem to have largely ended with the publication

A DISCOURSE ON METHOD *Sanford Kwinter*

2

of his book just after the war. But the basic duality was one that predated him and which continued after him to the present day. The duality I'm talking about is not the quantum duality—wave/particle or position/momentum—it is the duality between seeing life on one hand as a problem of mere transcription and reading out of a code, and on the other of deep, active correlation and emergence.

The best way to understand the ongoing conundrum of where form comes from is perhaps to consider how a contemporary theoretical biologist, Stuart Kauffman, describes it. In his book of a few years ago, *Investigations*, Kauffman sides very clearly with the holists. Against the dominant theory of the origin of life through the chance emergence of template molecules through which replication can take place, Kauffman proposes that life arose by means of confederacies of chemical networks whose coordinated activities mutually engendered the materials, shapes and forms they each respectively required. He evokes a very simple class of chemical system that any laboratory can assemble, in which two or more chemicals react with one another to produce a third chemical, which in turn reacts with a fourth chemical, which might well produce one of the original two reacting chemicals so that their reaction chain will begin all over again. This very simple system is called an autocatalytic loop. Kauffman speculates that life might well have begun from, and could well be explained as the product of, "collective autocatalytic sets."

To simplify all of this: The central problem of life is the problem of how matter came to organize itself to produce autonomous, stable entities that are self-directing. Also central to the problem of life is the problem of where form comes from. The tendency among reductionist biologists is to imagine that genetic processes can account for these things. In the end however, it has been shown that the genes are very unlikely candidates to fully explain these phenomena.

One of the most interesting and no doubt one of the most important developments of recent decades has been the move in biological sciences

A

A DISCOURSE ON METHOD   *Sanford Kwinter*

There is of course a profound, but also disconcerting, resemblance between the new work and the theoretical biology diagrams presented above, which were in wide circulation in architecture circles in the 1990s. These types of "isomorphism"—literal physical resemblances—have always been misleading, if not downright treacherous. And if there is any field that owes the model due respect for its integrity as a form of knowledge and communication, it is the field of architecture. Indeed the hugely augmented profile of architecture in the last decade and a half owes much to its status as a field of geometrical expertise and geometrical language, in an age in which knowledge has become increasingly deployed and articulated in qualitative, or modeling terms. The lucidity of the geometrical demonstrations by our two biologists represent enormously significant milestones in the history of thought, and open up a world of questions that our new century has just begun to address. Architecture was only a few years ago a central player in that game. Among the developments that have taken place of late, however, are a turn away from the agora of ideas, a rebellion against intellectualism perhaps, a renunciation of the larger issues that only the habits of critical engagement can capture, and a severe loss of seriousness in discourse and research. For many, the encounter with the world outside of but adjacent to academic and parochial architecture, with philosophy for example, with sociology and of course with the hard sciences as well, was too great a challenge and too distracting from the so-called "business of building."

Nevertheless, not only our field, but the world itself is at a crossroads, and the engagement with larger questions, even if only to coherently guide the energies of production, must not be treated merely as an occasional historical luxury or a spout that can be turned off at will. Our field cannot now back away from the cosmopolitan challenge taken on in the last decade, but currently obscured by the din of middlebrow critics and the facile and reflexive overproduction in the media and in our schools. Architectural ambition and architectural thought are inseparable. The search for models is what we are about.

48

METHODOLOGY   Historical Case Study

THE INVENTION OF THE URBAN RESEARCH STUDIO:
ROBERT VENTURI, DENISE SCOTT BROWN, AND STEVEN
IZENOUR'S *LEARNING FROM LAS VEGAS,* 1972

Martino Stierli

When they published their seminal study on the urbanism of the car-oriented city in 1972, American architects Robert Venturi, Denise Scott Brown, and Steven Izenour triggered a debate that was to shape architectural discourse for the following decade. By redefining architecture as a communication system, they thoroughly questioned the tenets of late modernism. *Learning from Las Vegas* was indeed taken as a provocation. While critics such as Tomas Maldonado and Kenneth Frampton accused the Venturi team of cynicism, cultural theorists welcomed the book as a manifesto of postmodernism, an appraisal Venturi and Scott Brown rather unsuccessfully attempted to reject. *Learning from Las Vegas* called for a renewal of architecture based on the methods first exploited by Pop Art, that is, a translation of the imagery of popular culture into a high-cultural context. Thus, the Venturi team took the commercial vernacular of the American city as a visual repository out of which a socially and aesthetically relevant contemporary architecture should evolve.

Learning from Las Vegas, irrespective of the heated debates it initiated, also comprised a highly innovative experiment in architectural education. The book was based on a programmatic essay that Venturi and Scott Brown had published in *Architectural Forum* in 1968 and on a research studio they tutored jointly at Yale University in the fall of the same year, with their assistant Steven Izenour. The Las Vegas studio was one in a series of three consecutive courses Venturi and Scott Brown taught at Yale, each of which was directed at investigating new methods of architectural education and learning. Both Venturi and Scott Brown had been independently involved in instruction at a number of universities, but it was at Yale that they amalgamated their ideas into a coherent approach to architectural education. In 1967, they and their students had investigated the architecture and signage in metropolitan mass-transportation systems. In 1970, the "Learning from Levittown" studio focused on the imagery of the private realms of suburban homeowners. This study was informed by a sociological understanding of the everyday suburban landscape.

All three studios and the Las Vegas one in particular were unusual both in content and methodology. As their object, the studios took the layout and appearance of the suburban, car-oriented landscape of "urban sprawl." They proceeded along the disciplinary divide between architecture and urban planning, seeking to analyze and dissect the contemporary city while at the same time specifically addressing the consequences of the findings for architectural design. More importantly, the studios departed from the traditional design studio to make research the main focus of their investigation. A large part of the semester program was taken up by library research and a field trip to Las Vegas. The main objective of this inquiry was to arrive at a valid image of the urban form which had developed in the American West and whose significance for contemporary culture had been asserted a few years earlier by writer Tom Wolfe. To this end, the Venturi team and their students experimented with a variety of visual media. In addition to relatively conventional media such as maps and charts, photography and film took a prominent part in their research. By mounting a camera on the hood of their car and driving along the Strip (a technique borrowed from artist Ed Ruscha), the Venturi team recorded an unadulterated or in their terms "deadpan" image of the city.

The "Learning from Las Vegas" studio was the prototype for a number of subsequent attempts to accommodate urban research within architectural education, in particular in its use of new representational media to analyze the city. However, for Venturi and Scott Brown, research did not constitute an end in itself. Rather, the analytical and scholarly approach was intended to form a basis for architectural production, and Venturi and Scott Brown emphasized the fact that their studios were directed toward designers. Referring to methods developed in the humanities and empirical sociology, they introduced the notion of interdisciplinary discourse into architectural education. By presenting visual media as the object and product of research, they demonstrated the mutual applicability of science and the arts and the informative potential of this application for architectural design.

BIBLIOGRAPHY
• Golec, Michael, and Aaron Vinegar (eds.). "Instruction and Provocation, or Relearning from Las Vegas," *Visible Language* 37 (2003), no. 3 (special issue).
• Moos, Stanislaus von. *Venturi, Rauch & Scott Brown.* New York: Rizzoli, 1987.
• Scott Brown, Denise. *Urban Concepts.* London/New York: Academy Editions/St. Martin's Press, 1990.
• Stierli, Martino. "Ins Bild gerückt. Ästhetik, Form und Diskurs der Stadt in Venturis und Scott Browns *Learning from Las Vegas*." Dissertation, ETH Zürich, 2007.
• Venturi, Robert, Denise Scott Brown, and Steven Izenour. *Learning from Las Vegas.* Cambridge, Mass./London: MIT Press, 1972.

49

A VENTURI, SCOTT BROWN, IZENOUR *Martino Stierli*

1,2   Imaging the city: Students
of the Learning from Las Vegas research
studio preparing a camera for filming
on the Las Vegas Strip and on Fremont
Street, 1968.

3   A "deadpan" image of Las
Vegas: Sequence of stills from a film
taken with a motorized camera,
documenting a drive on the Las Vegas
Strip, 1968.

4   "A schedule of Las Vegas Strip
hotels: Plans and sections and elements":
chart from the first edition of *Learning
from Las Vegas,* 1972.

1

2

3

4

LAPA

Laboratoire de la production d'architecture
Ecole Polytechnique Fédérale de Lausanne (EPFL)

Harry Gugger
Ralph Blättler
Thomas Bregman
Simon Chessex
Ning Liu
Russell Loveridge
John Morgan
Pascale Luck Quattrocci
Antoine Robert-Grandpierre
Henriette Spoerl

FROM CITY TO DETAIL: THE SPHERE OF THE ARCHITECT

Harry Gugger and Carolin Stapenhorst

The sphere of the architect is shrinking: today architecture finds itself in the paradoxical situation of being more popular than ever before, of getting enormous media attention, while at the same time being exposed to total decline. On the one hand architecture has become the media of many: developers, investors, cooperations, institutions, and on the other hand most construction happens without architects. Architectural design is being influenced by an ever-greater number of skills and interests, as a result of which architects become marginalized.

To cope with this problem, the EPFL's Laboratory of Architectural Production (LAPA) has developed and teaches a working and design methodology primarily aimed at ensuring that architects continue to play a central, coordinating and integrative part in the design process.

LAPA's name reflects its didactic and scientific orientation: it is a laboratory, a place of applied research, dedicated to the analysis and development of design processes. As a system, it is just as concerned with the process as with its result, the designed project.

The term production refers to LAPA's approach, in which the built environment is defined as the product of an intellectual, artistic, technical and mechanized process encompassing both design and material execution as well as use and maintenance. The different phases of this process correspond to the classifications used by many professional associations. LAPA aims to expand the architect's sphere of influence with a view to increasing control over the quality of its production, that is, architecture.

A DIGITAL CONNECTION OF CONCEPT AND PRODUCT
LAPA has therefore developed a methodology that prepares students to operate within an interdisciplinary framework and examines the use of digital technologies to optimize artistic and productive processes. Taking a focus on interdisciplinarity, the life cycle of a building, and the rationalization of productive processes as a basis, LAPA identifies, lists and streamlines the parameters that influence the design process and the outcome. Formal investigations go hand in hand with research into such key factors as social, economic, political and legal conditions, environmental and contextual parameters, and technological and constructive systems. An examination of the relationships and relative weights of these factors yields an overview of the complexity of the design process. By this approach, scientific methods are combined with artistic explorations, making urban and architectural design an investigative process. LAPA also builds a bridge to the

professional world by involving external participants such as public institutions or industry representatives in its projects each year, enriching its own production with new perspectives. In this way, the sphere of investigation is expanded, more factors are taken into consideration, and the interdisciplinary approach is fleshed out.

A distinct part of the process is dedicated to researching the application of digital technologies, such as generative CAD programs or computer-aided manu-facturing (CAM). The goal is to escape formalism and to efficiently streamline and coordinate the flow of data. LAPA's research in this area attempts to create a direct digital connection between concept and construction that is thoroughly controlled by architects.

STUDIO WORK IN INTERDISCIPLINARY GROUPS

LAPA's design studio runs a full academic year. Each year a new location of schol-arly interest is chosen. The first semester is dedicated to the development of the Urban Constitution (UC), which consists of a constitutional text and a strate-gic development plan. The Urban Constitution covers a large scale urban area. Based on the guidelines of the UC a series of architectural projects are devel-oped in the second semester. These projects test the viability of the objectives and measures defined by the UC.

The first semester of the course follows a specific organizational structure whereby each participating student is assigned a role in two different types of groups: each student is part of a group of five designers, the design team, which concentrates on planning and spatial conceptualization, and is concurrently a member of a specialist group, which addresses specific design-related topics. The design teams present the results of urban design, while the specialist groups develop strategies for topics such as environment, health, education, transport, food and housing. Each design team consists of the different special-ists, who become experts in their topic and advisors to their design team. In this way, design activities are carried out jointly in an interdisciplinary group with various skills.

Urban planning in the first semester is organized in three assignments, with students performing their duties in both types of groups. The first assignment asks the design teams to develop a case study to portray related typologies of the planning area and analyze contributions from the various special topics as well as a selection of statistical and physical base data. For the second assign-ment, the specialist groups develop urban strategies for their specific topics, which form an interdisciplinary basis for further planning, and are superimposed in the next assignment to form the urban constitution, which is again worked on by the design team. The Urban Constitution provides a logical set of guiding rules that allow for an appropriate and consistent response to changing urban and societal needs. It becomes the planning foundation for the entire remaining course.

THE MAKING OF THE PROOF OF CONCEPT

During the first assignment of the second semester, either individual students or pairs choose locations and programs for architectural design in the planning area. In the form of a feasibility study, program requirements are tested for their compatibility with the location. A diagrammatic concept design and a brief are developed to form the basis for the architectural project. Depending on their specific program, students consult external experts and deepen the interdisciplinary aspect of the design. Using digital technology, they develop and fine-tune their work, from schematic design to the final presentation documentation. In the second semester, the students are in a complex, non-linear stage of the design process, which they continually document. LAPA finds itself in the paradoxical situation where it uses the traditional phasing models as a didactical concept only to teach their students to apply a more complex and itinerate method of design and production. The extensive use of information technologies, and as a consequence the digital chain, allow for immediate jumps between concept an product and transform the traditional layers of presentation or make them completely redundant. The student designs achieve a high degree of detail, describing materiality, structure, and construction systems. By means of digital technology, students are able to produce mock-ups and construction details all the way to a scale of 1:1.

DESIGN TEAMS AND SPECIALIST GROUPS

	Specialist Group 1	Specialist Group 2	Specialist Group 3	Specialist Group 4	Specialist Group 5	
DESIGN TEAM 1	FOOD	HEALTH	EDUCATION	HABITAT	TRANSPORT	URBAN CONSTITUTION 1
DESIGN TEAM 2	FOOD	HEALTH	EDUCATION	HABITAT	TRANSPORT	URBAN CONSTITUTION 2
DESIGN TEAM 3	FOOD	HEALTH	EDUCATION	HABITAT	TRANSPORT	URBAN CONSTITUTION 3
DESIGN TEAM 4	FOOD	HEALTH	EDUCATION	HABITAT	TRANSPORT	URBAN CONSTITUTION 4
DESIGN TEAM 5	FOOD	HEALTH	EDUCATION	HABITAT	TRANSPORT	URBAN CONSTITUTION 5
	Strategy Group 1	Strategy Group 2	Strategy Group 3	Strategy Group 4	Strategy Group 5	

DESIGN PHASES

PRODUCTION PROCESS									
SIA	Strategic planning	Preliminary studies	Project			Invitation to bid	Implementation		Management
RIBA	Feasibility studies	Outline design	Scheme design	Detail design	Production information	Tender action	Project planning	Site operations	Feed back
AIA	Pre-design	Site analysis	Schematic design	Design development	Contract documents	Bidding or negotiations	Contract administration		Post-contract services
Loi MOP	Esquisse	Avant-projet sommaire	Avant-projet définitif	Projet	Contrat de travaux	Exécution et examen	Direction de l'exécution	Pilotage de chantier	Réception
LAPA	Feasibility study	Schematic design		Design development	Construction documentation		Presentation documentation		

ARCHITECTS ACTUAL FIELD OF INFLUENCE

ARCHITECTS EXPANDED FIELD OF INFLUENCE

FIRST SEMESTER:
URBAN SCALE

In the first semester, the investigation on urban scale is structured in three phases: Case Studies, Urban Strategies and Urban Constitution.

I   CASE STUDY
The site of investigation is put into context through comparative Case Studies. Case Study topics are chosen to create understanding of the specificities of the investigated site in its larger context. A set of five research themes guides exploration of the Case Studies. These themes are derived from the particular situation of the site of investigation. The report on each case is a compilation of the five research themes along with standardized statistical and physical data and an overall analysis and set of conclusions. The conclusions clarify the particularities of the site and identify exemplary features or policies.

II   URBAN STRATEGY
Once the Case Studies are compiled and the results evaluated, the focus of investigation shifts to the selected site. For the Urban Strategies, each participant assumes the role of a "specialist" conducting research and analysis on one of the defined themes. The themes are chosen for the vital role they play for the site. The "specialists" begin by investigating the site and compiling statistics, data and geographic information for analysis. Once the basic data has been compiled, the "specialists" work in consultation with each other to develop a strategic plan for their theme.

III   URBAN CONSTITUTION
The results of the Case Studies and Urban Strategy are reflected in the development of an Urban Constitution for the site, which provides a logical set of guiding rules that allow for an appropriate and consistent response to changing urban and societal needs. The Urban Constitution addresses the perceived local needs in the short, medium and long term, and is represented as a schematic strategy that integrates the multiple overlapping aspects of planning. The Urban Constitution consists of two elements: a constitution text and a strategic development plan which translates the objectives of the constitution into a planning document.

SECOND SEMESTER:
PROJECT SCALE

Based on the guidelines of the Urban Constitution, a series of architectural projects are developed as a "proof of concept," testing the viability of the objectives and measures defined by the Urban Constitution. The architectural project must respect, adapt and, at the same time, substantiate the conditions imposed on individual sites. The sheer number of interventions allows extrapolating the final stage of the future shape of the overall site. The development of the project is structured in five design phases: feasibility study, schematic design, detailed design, construction documents and presentation documents.

IV   FEASIBILITY STUDY
During this phase it is required to devise a project brief, choose a site within the Urban Constitution and prepare studies to assess the feasibility of the project within the set guidelines, which will furthermore lead the project development. The feasibility study should outline the current physical, infrastructural and legal conditions and restrictions of a site and develop a diagrammatic approach to assessing its compatibility with the program of the proposed brief.

V   SCHEMATIC DESIGN
The schematic design transforms the diagrammatic descriptions of the feasibility study into a functional, logical and aesthetic design concept. The contextual issues of the site, other proposed projects and connections are addressed, and solutions for basic issues of structure, materials, overall aesthetics and volumetric relationships are explored. Most importantly, the schematic design is the point at which an identifiable architectural expression of the project is formulated and strategies for the primary issues of function, infrastructure, materiality and construction are devised.

VI   DESIGN DEVELOPMENT
The design development is the refinement of the schematic design to improve functionality and to develop the details of the design. This process finalizes the design integration of larger issues of structure, materiality, construction systems and subsystems. The project idea is strengthened by completing and refining the design on all scales and by generating expressive or appropriate details that will guide the process of deciding on the techniques and technologies to be employed for fabrication and construction.

VII   CONSTRUCTION DOCUMENTATION
Construction documents are the primary product from an architect, both in terms of output and information. CAD drawings of plan, section and elevation or isometric drawings are therefore developed, as required for tender to a primary building contractor or a component supplier. The creation of a different set of construction documents using alternative digital CD concepts such as Computer Aided Manufacturing or Parametric Design is encouraged and supported.

VIII   PRESENTATION DOCUMENTATION
The presentation documentation describes the entire project from feasibility study to the final design and construction process and primarily addresses the following issues:
- The design, program, and implementation of the architectural project within the existing context in keeping with the overall goals of the Urban Constitution.
- The fabrication of mock-ups and construction samples in order to get an accurate sense of how the building will be built and what its actual character will be at the 1:1 scale.

#1
CAMPUS OR CONCEPT OF METABOLISM, 2005/06
LAPA's inaugural project was an investigation of its own environment, the campus of the Swiss Federal Institute of Technology (EPFL) and the University of Lausanne (UNIL) and the neighboring communities

#2
HAVANA, 10 DE OCTUBRE (10DE10) 2006/07
The academic year 2006/07 was dedicated to the re-qualification of the municipality "10 de Octubre" in Havana, Cuba. The following illustrations of LAPA's methodology are samples from this investigation.

#3
LONDON SOUTHWARK 2007/08
In the past academic year LAPA checked the feasibility of the London Plan, specifically its request for an additional 29,000 housing units by 2016 in the London Borough of Southwark

I   CASE STUDY
      10DE10, Metropolitan Growth
Havana's size and population have not consid-
erably increased since 1959, while massive
urban development can be observed in other
cities examined, such as Caracas, Mexico City,
or Miami. The Cuban decentralization policy,
resolutely applied after the revolution in 1959,
favored the increase of population in medium-
sized to small towns and rural regions.
The chart highlights the exceptional character
of Havana's almost unchanging urban figure
since the 1950s.

HAVANA
Population 2,168,255
(ONE 2006)

MIAMI
Population 2,253,362
(PMSA 2000)

CARACAS
Population more than
2,700,000
(Censo Nacional 2001)

MEXICO CITY
Population 19,311,365
(INEGI 2005)

1800

1900

1940

1960

2007

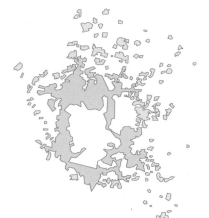

II   URBAN STRATEGY
10DE10, Theme: Health
Extracts from presentation of a strategy to improve health care provision in the municipality 10DE10.

1–4   Presentation of one localized problem: lack of means for emergency transport.
5   Proposition aims at minimal investment cost and immediate feasibility: installation of a network of basic rescue centers to shorten the response time of emergency transport.

6   Establishment of a fast lane for emergency transport connecting hospitals and rescue centers using secondary streets, in good condition, with no major intersections.

1

Polyclinics in Diez De Octubre

Surgery Clinics and Research Hospitals

Pharmacies

Family Doctor Offices

Other health care services well distributed? Usually.

2

LESS PEOPLE DIE IN LAUSANNE FROM ACCIDENTS THAN IN DIEZ DE OCTUBRE.

WHY?

DIEZ DE OCTUBRE
LAUSANNE

Deaths due to accidents per 100'000 inhabitants

3

Lausanne

Diez de Octubre

Does Lausanne have more hospitals to keep people alive? Not at all.

4

Lausanne (existing)   Ambulance

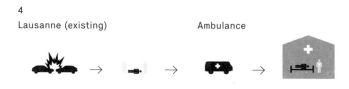

Diez de Octubre (existing)

Diez de Octubre (proposal)   [A] First Aid Station   [B] Hospital

5

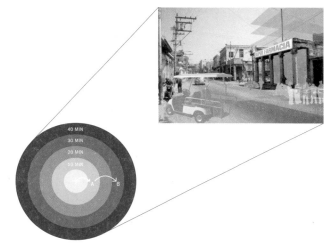

6

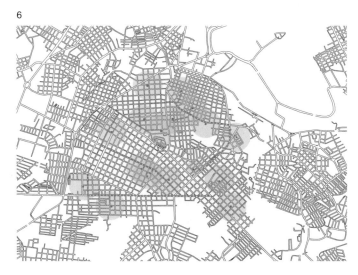

III   URBAN CONSTITUTION
       1ODE1O, Constitution Text
HAVANA'S FUTURE: The opening chapter of the
urban constitution states the overall objectives
for the development of the research area's larger
context, in this case the city of Havana.

1ODE1O UC / HAVANA'S FUTURE

1   URBAN HUB FOR KNOWLEDGE AND ARTS SOCIETY
- port of trade for knowledge and goods
- melting pot for spanish Speaking societies from North and South America and the Carribbean
- city of arts and culture

2   POLY-CENTRIC METROPOLIS
- create self-sufficient subcenters in tune with the different urban structures and their specific history, would also serve as key measure to reduce traffic and create greater balance of service distribution across the city

3   TRANSFORM THE BAY
- harbur is no more the key function of the bay
- the bay acts as the city's water park and attracts multiple functions (sports, leisure, housing, business services)

4   TRADE AND WORK THE BRAND
- Havana has a unique urban quality to offer
- profit from the historical heritage, maintain and strengthen the image of a city for arts and culture, improve global network
- further establish Havana as knowledge hub with focus on healthcare and education

5   ACKNOWLEDGE KEY ROLE FOR CUBA
- Havana is the ambassador for Cuba
- Havana has to offer international standards
- invest in the city's and connecting infrastructure
- unique compactness combined with qualified transportation system will lead to highly efficient urban structure

6   INVESTIGATE SCENARIO OF GROWTH
- profit from the unique situation of a highly controlled planning environment
- qualified and controlled growth, within the existing structures and on the bay, to be considered in light of potential migration of qualified workforce from abroad

FACTS AND FIGURES: The second chapter introduces the main facts about the research area, in this case the municipality 10 de Octubre (10DE10), addressed by the proposals of the urban constitution.

GENERAL PROPOSALS: The third chapter states the general objectives for development of the research area, which are further elaborated in subsequent chapters.

10DE10 UC / GENERAL PROPOSALS

1   10DE10 CAN NOT ONLY BE REHABILITATED, IT NEEDS TO BE REINVENTED
- make 10de10 a strong and self-sufficient subcenter of Havana

2   KEEP THE DENSITY
- use opportunities to create more public and private open space

3   CREATE MULTIFUNCTIONAL AND POLY-CENTRIC TOWN
- enhance the structural identities of the different neighborhoods (Luyano; Santos Suarez; Vibora and Lawton)
- add varied functions of local, national and international scale

4   MAKE USE OF STRATEGIC LOCATION
- create new major north-south connections
- use the redevelopment of the harbor to bring 10de10 to the bay
- transform Via Blanca from a boundary to a link with the bay and central Havana

5   PROFIT FROM HISTORICAL ROOTS
- reestablish 10de10 as a place for subculture, artists' community, intellects' playground

6   USE TOPOGRAPHY AS A PROMOTING FACTOR
- topography differentiates 10de10 from other municipalities
- make use of good climatic conditions
- Loma offers a potential for symbolic landmarks

HABITAT, HEALTH, FOOD, EDUCATION,
TRANSPORT: The constitution text goes into
further detail, and describes the development
goals that have been isolated for the different
research themes in the chapters Habitat, Health,
Food, Education, and Transport.

10DE10 UC / HABITAT

1   TRANSFORM FROM A LIVING TO A MULTIFUNCTIONAL CITY
- injection of new program in addition to rehabilitation is inevitable and will request tough planning measures

2   KEEP THE DENSITY BUT CREATE VARIETY OF DENSITY
- increase density in strategic locations such as: gateways, open spaces, main circulation axis, subcenters and on the interface with the bay (Luyano)

3   CREATE DIFFERENCES AND VARIETY
- make 10de10 a workplace for the production of services, knowledge and food

4   CREATE GATEWAYS AND ADD NEW SUB-CENTERS
- use new north-south connections (Porvenir and Serrano) as linear service districts
- use the harbor area, Loma del Chaplet, Tramvia depot, Convento Santa Clara for central public functions
- use the transport intersections for the creation of gateways to 10de10

5   REHABILITATE THE HISTORICAL HERITAGE
- form and function to be kept in tune
- maintain 10de10 as a place for subculture, artists' community, intellects' playground

10DE10 UC / HEALTH

1   HEALTH SERVICES
- maintain excellent current distribution of general services
- improve specific services such as ambulance
- renovate and renew the existing facilities
- add centers of excellence

2   HYGIENIC ISSUES
- improve water supply system
- establish state of the art sewage system
- create retention system for flooding emergencies
- establish waste management with focus on recycling and energy production

3   ENVIRONMENTAL ISSUES
- make 10de10 a municipality with an exemplary carbon footprint
- trigger use of renewable energy, e.g. solar energy, biomass energy

1ODE1O UC / FOOD

1　URBAN AGRICULTURE
- develop urban agriculture further
- create positive image through education
- produce nutrition and medical plants
- avoid fertilizer, promote biological production
- test breading of animals
- enhance urban and architectural quality of agriculture

2　RETAIL
- maintain current distribution of services
- avoid concentration and centralization of services
- enhance variety in size and content
- link fresh product production with close-by selling opportunities

3　CATERING
- trigger the creation of a variety of eating places

1ODE1O UC / EDUCATION

1　MAINTAIN EXCELLENT DISTRIBUTION OF SERVICES
- avoid concentration

2　MAINTAIN EXISTING FACILITIES
- acknowledge need for rehabilitation

3　CREATE SYNERGIES AND SUB CENTERS
- manage and operate different institutions centrally, e.g. Casa de Cultura, primary and secondary school

4　CREATE CENTERS OF EXCELLENCE
- add institutions of national and international character, e.g. University Loma del Chaplet

10DE10 UC/TRANSPORT

1 **KEEP THE STREETS AS LIVING ROOM FOR HABANEROS**
 - transportation is just one function of the street
 - enhance function as strolling- and play-ground

2 **FAVOR PEDESTRIAN CIRCULATION**
 - create appropriate sidewalks
 - deprivatize colonnades
 - provide shadow by planting trees

3 **ENHANCE PUBLIC TRANSPORT**
 - create synergies between rail and road
 - establish railways around 10de10 with new stations connecting to bus routes
 - establish transportation hubs and gateways

4 **DISTRIBUTE AND KEEP LOW PRIVATE TRAFFIC**
 - create new major north-south links to de-stress situation in Calzada 10de10
 - establish typologies of road profiles in view of minimizing impact of private traffic
 - depending on further evolution consider traffic toll to support park+ride

5 **CHANNEL HEAVY TRAFFIC**
 - create consolidation centers at gateways and transportation hubs
 - manage and operate deliveries via specific routes at restricted times

6 **PROMOTE CYCLING**
 - change negative image related to the "periodo especial"
 - introduce bicycle routes

7 **BE PREPARED FOR POTENTIAL PARKING PROBLEMS**
 - define strategies to keep the parking away from the street
 - apply existing references of parking and maintenance centers create park+ride at gateways

III   URBAN CONSTITUTION
      10DE10, Strategic Development Plan
The zoning plan translates the Urban Constitution into a planning tool. Objectives such as
densification, differentiation, change of occu-
pation, new development, etc. are codified in
the zoning plan. The plan serves as planning
basis for the development of the subsequent
architectural interventions.

1   Zoning Plan for 10DE10

    Health
    Housing
    Industries
    Education
    Culture
    Commercial
    Office
    Sport Area
    Green Space
    Urban Agriculture
    Market
    Parking
    Multifunction
    Square

1

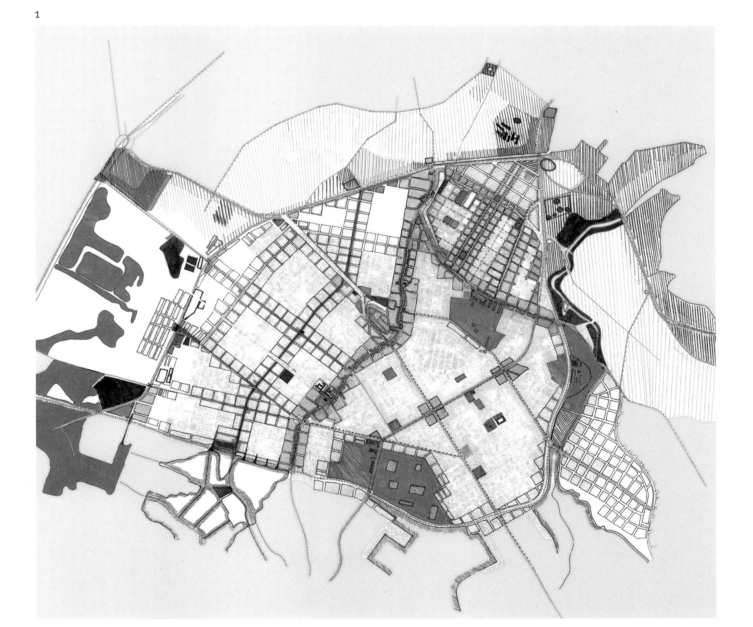

ARCHITECTURE INJECTION
10DE10, Map of architectural projects:
Different sites are chosen and relevant programs conceived by the student teams, based
on the requirements of the urban constitution
and in accordance with the planning guidelines
of the Strategic Development Plan.

1   Plan of municipality 10 de Octubre
with project sites.
A   MARKET AND HOUSING
Lucas Cohen-Adad, Melanie Monks
B   CONVENTION CENTER
Carmen Ebneter, Mio Tsuneyama
C   DANCE SCHOOL
Marnie Amato, Nicole Giambonini
D   LIVE/WORK UNITS
Jérémy Trieu
E   THEATER
Joana Varela, Alexandre Vergères
F   SCHOOL
Nadine Schmied
G   CIUDAD DE LA MUSICA
Miguel Marques

H   SWIMMING POOL
Isabel Oliveira
I   WATER STRUCTURE
Florian Chazeau
J   LIBRARY
Wing-Chung Cheung, Léonard Gurtner
K   RECYCLING CENTER
Julien Ecoffrey, Frédéric Karam
L   CASA DE CULTURA
Deborah Eker
M   BRIDGE/TRAIN STATION
Maxime Duvoisin
N   TRAIN/FIRE STATION
Nathanael Chollet, Yann Gramegna

1

IV   FEASIBILITY STUDY
     Water Structure, 10DE10
Studies to define the scale and location of the
proposed program for a Water Structure
2   Feasibility study for an implementation of:
     a   a series of medium-size structures
providing constant access to drinking water for
the immediate neighborhoods
     b   for a large scale structure serving the
whole municipality

3   Parameters for the location of the
Water Structure:
     a   Site on natural elevation using the
height difference to produce necessary water
pressure
     b   Choice of prominent location to pro-
duce new landmark
     c   Implementation adjacent to public
green space to create synergies between additional public programs offered within the water
structure and the existing public amenities

2a

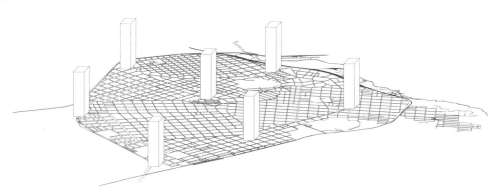

2b

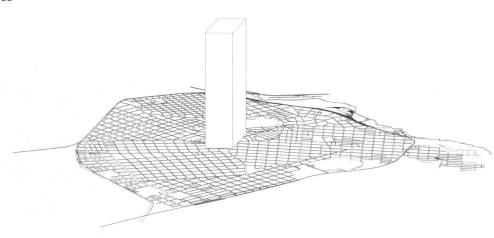

3a   3b   3c

V   SCHEMATIC DESIGN
     10DE10, Water Structure
Further development of functional proposal:
combination of primary function (water storage)
and secondary program (context related:
shops, recreation, workplaces…).
   1a   Water Tower
   1b   Fixed Program
   1c   Contextual Program

2a   Water Structure
▨▨▨▨   Water Tower program
– underground tank 400m³
– main tank 600m³
▮▮▮   Fixed program
– food store 60m²
– post office 50m²
– bakery 50m²
▮▮▮   Fixed program
– external terrace 400m²
▮▮▮   Fixed program
– bodega 200m²
▮▮▮   Contextual program
– water office management 1600m²

2b   Contextual program, water office
management 1600m².
3   Schematic design proposal: Conventional structure of water reservoir with added
layer of usable spaces, circulation along the
outer perimeter of the structure.
4   Sketch rendering of proposed
structure.

1a   1b   1c   2a   2b

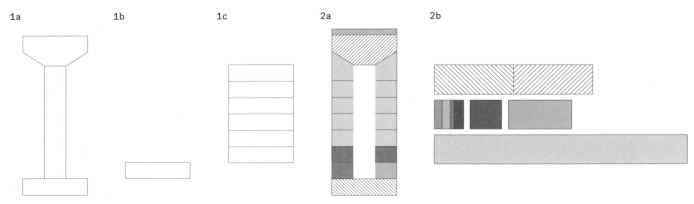

3   4

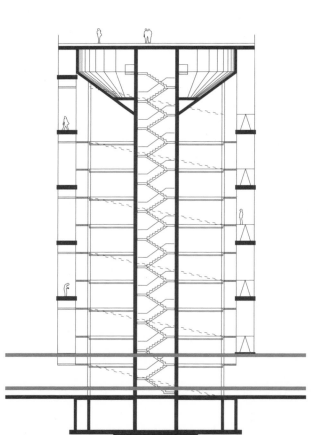

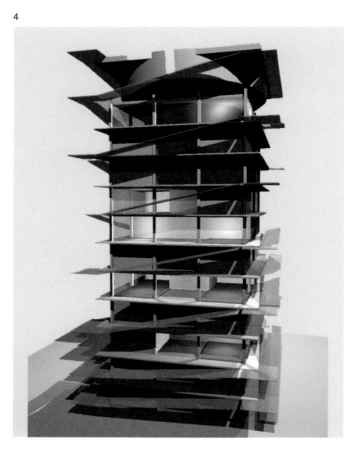

VI   DESIGN DEVELOPMENT
     10DE10, Water Structure

5   Schematic Drawing of possible organization principles: Conventional layout with elongated funnel for water storage, added functions on the outside. Water storage at the external face of the building, enclosed spaces for other functions.

6   Design proposal of a circular, uniform structure.

5

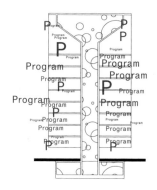
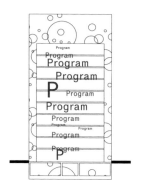

6

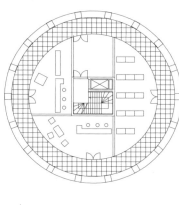
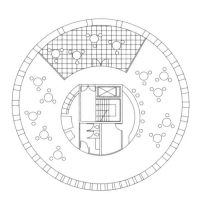
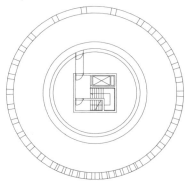
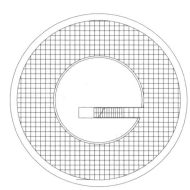

VII   CONSTRUCTION DOCUMENTATION
       10DE10, Water Structure
1   Development of facade modules,
different types and functionalities of units
  1a   Water module
  1b   Solar panel module
  1c   *Moucharabieh*

2   Illustration of assembly principle for
facade modules, test of a new geometry
3   Illustration of assembly principle for
facade modules, east & west elevations,
module type B (1.45m)

1

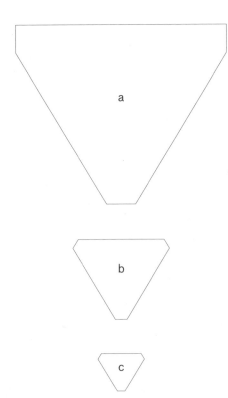

2

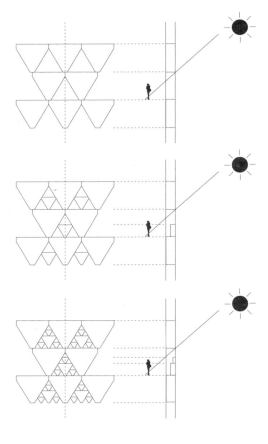

3

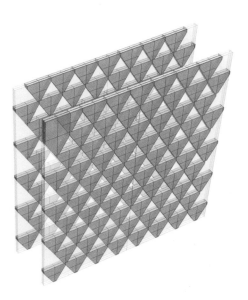

VIII   PRESENTATION DOCUMENTATION
10DE10, Water Structure
4   Schematic presentation of construction principle, modular wall, large scale structural beams and floor slabs

5   Sections of the final project

4

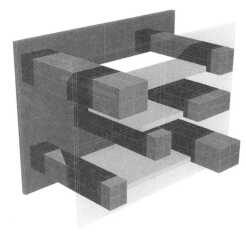

5

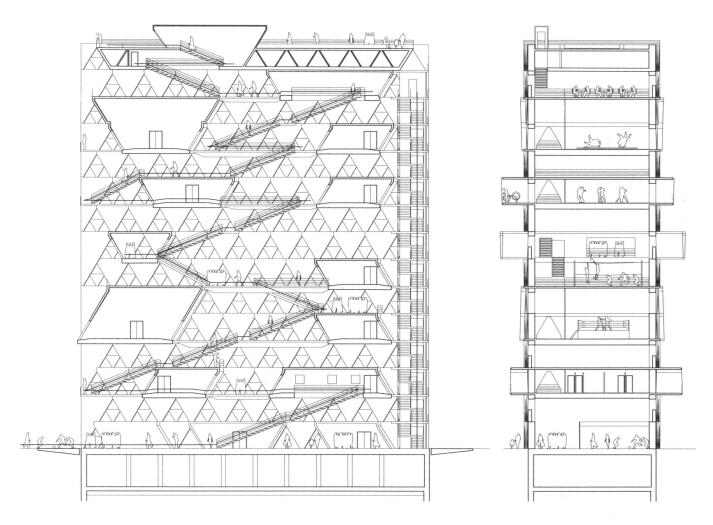

10DE10 Water Structure [I]
    1   Overall Perspective
    2   Illustration of additional programs:
    a   Ballroom
    b   Volleyball field

1

2a

2b

PROJECTS
Examples from 10DE10
    3   Ciudad de la Musica [G]
    4   Library [J]
    5   Fire/Train Station [N]
    6   Recycling Center [K]
    7   Theater [E]

3

4

5

6

7

B

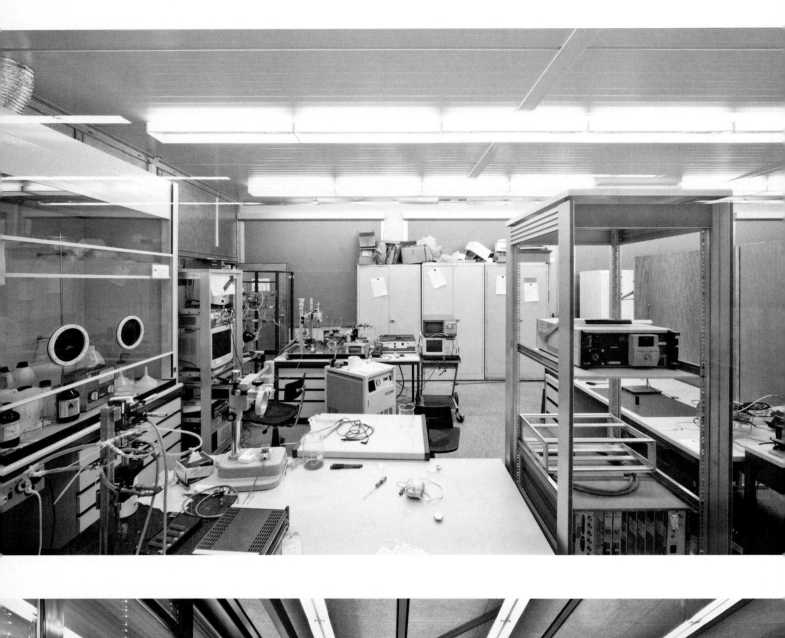

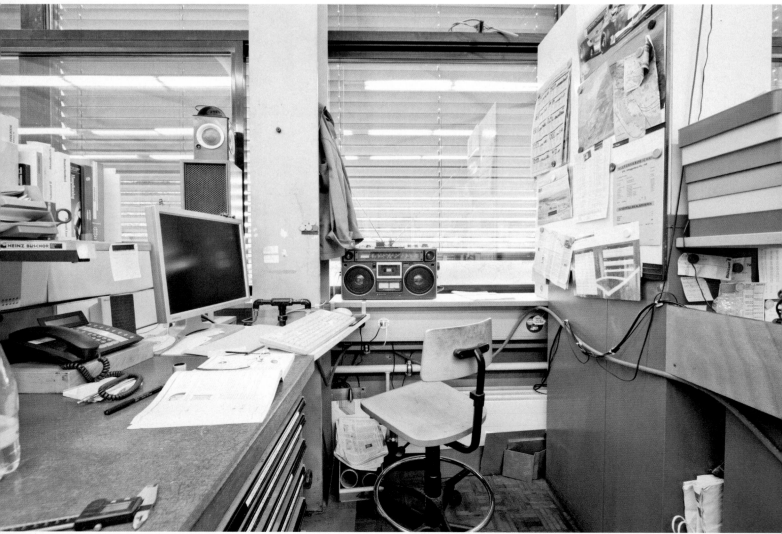

B

NETWORKS

CRITICAL PRACTICE BETWEEN SCIENCE AND ART:
LUCIUS BURCKHARDT AND THE EMERGENCE OF
PLANNING THEORY

Martin Josephy

It is not seldom that trained architects change professions and even attain prominence in another métier. Lucius Burckhardt (1925–2003) took the opposite route. Studies in sociology and economics and a dissertation in political science gave him an unorthodox approach to design and planning questions, which ultimately led him to stake out a series of significant positions in the extensive field of urban planning, architecture and design. An enumeration of his most important engagements in teaching and research ought to be sufficient to illustrate, along this one line, how Burckhardt followed a branching path far beyond the academic domain. First, however, it is necessary to point out an essential commonality of these engagements: they were all located in the context of paradigmatic and structural upheavals.

In 1959, in the wake of the controversial debates brought on by the manifesto *achtung: die Schweiz*, Burckhardt was given a teaching position at the Hochschule für Gestaltung Ulm. Following the resignation of Max Bill, the school was going through a "phase of innovation" whereby the old Bauhaus doctrine was being replaced by a new concept of design grounded in scholarship and theory. A simple axiom that Burckhardt coined years later, "design is invisible," identifies the central theme of that time. In 1961, Burckhardt was appointed the first lecturer in sociology in the architecture department of ETH Zurich. But it would be an entire decade before this school, like the HfG Ulm, would also declare its "experimental phase," in the course of which he was made a visiting professor with his own design studio. In this position, the "Lehrcanapé" which he held from 1970 to 1973 with the successive accompaniment of credentialed architects Rolf Gutmann and Rainer Senn, thoughts on contemporary design and planning methods condensed into a robust critique of an institute model that, in adhering to a received design academicism, was incapable of creating a basis for taking on the "wicked problems" of an increasingly complex experience of the world. The demand for the "smallest possible intervention," for a teaching that made more reference to practice and a research oriented towards the humanities and social sciences, was not—as it was commonly understood—an attack on architecture itself, but rather on the conditions under which architecture is produced.

After the experiment at ETH Zurich, which was discontinued in 1973—and after ten years as editor of the magazine *Werk*—there followed a long-term engagement at the newly founded Gesamthochschule Kassel. There,

as professor of social economy of urban systems, Burckhardt was an essential participant in developing the department of architecture, landscape architecture and urban planning. At the Gesamthochschule, structural innovations, including interdisciplinary project-based studies and academic self-administration, were inseparably connected with the establishment of new content for teaching and research. However, Burckhardt was less oriented toward the Zeitgeist than he was toward a tradition of dialectic thought, as could be seen in the way he broke up discourses rather than consolidating them. In Kassel, in constant exchange with his wife, Annemarie, numerous colleagues and multiple generations of students, he produced relevant contributions to planning methodology, participation, historic preservation, ecology, and landscape aesthetics.

In retrospect, as a consequence of changed conditions in the university landscape, the demand for academic positioning seems to have then been made again. With gentle irony towards the institution, but with all due seriousness regarding the matter at hand, in the 1980s Burckhardt founded a new discipline, *strollology*, which aims to bring the concept of beauty up to date, among other concerns. Initially unfocussed and without a clear designation, this line of research can be traced back to a seminar in landscape theory and the subsequent walk, the "Voyage to Tahiti," which was staged on the outskirts of Kassel in a nature preserve that had been converted from a military training ground. The question that served as a point of departure, "what do discoverers discover?" also describes the scholarly attitude that Burckhardt put forward in his academic work: like the act of taking a stroll, which makes a chain of unrelated impressions into an entirety, teaching and research also involve taking fragmentary knowledge and organizing it in a new way, with a view towards a completed picture. The question of where new realizations are possible and how these can be placed was always of primary importance to Burckhardt. This also explains his conviction that, in all probability, certain perspectives can only be conveyed through art.

BIBLIOGRAPHY
• Burckhardt, Lucius. *Die Kinder fressen ihre Revolution. Wohnen – Planen – Bauen – Grünen.* Ed. by Bazon Brock. Köln: DuMont Buchverlag, 1985.
• ———. *Design ist unsichtbar.* Ed. by Hans Höger for Rat für Formgebung. Ostfildern: Cantz Verlag, 1995.
• ———. *Wer plant die Planung? Architektur, Politik und Mensch.* Ed. by Jesko Fezer and Martin Schmitz. Berlin: Martin Schmitz Verlag, 2004.
• ———. *Warum ist Landschaft schön? Die Spaziergangs- wissenschaft.* Ed. by Markus Ritter and Martin Schmitz. Berlin: Martin Schmitz Verlag, 2006.
• Burckhardt, Lucius, and Walter Maria Förderer. *Bauen ein Prozess.* Teufen: Arthur Niggli, 1968.
• Burckhardt, Lucius, Max Frisch, and Markus Kutter. *Achtung: die Schweiz. Ein Gespräch über unsere Lage und ein Vorschlag zur Tat.* Basel: Verlag F. Handschin, 1955.

B   LUCIUS BURCKHARDT   *Martin Josephy*

1,2   Happening on the occasion of the international workshop "Denkmalpflege ist Sozialpolitik" (Historic Preservation is Social Policy), Kassel, 1975, photo: Beat Schweingruber

3   Lucius Burckhardt with his students at the Wilhelmshöhe hillside park in Kassel, photo: Linde Burkhardt
4   "0 m—The Origin of the Landscape," installation by French artist Paul-Armand Gette on invitation of

Lucius Burckhardt, Kassel, 1985, photo: Monika Nikolic
5   "Voyage to Tahiti," public walk at the Dönche nature reserve in Kassel, 1987, photo: Klaus Hoppe

1

2

3

4

5

NETWORKS

Essay

1

"GIVE ME A GUN AND I WILL MAKE ALL BUILDINGS MOVE":
AN ANT'S VIEW OF ARCHITECTURE

Bruno Latour, Albena Yaneva

Our building problem is just the opposite of Etienne Jules Marey's famous inquiry into the physiology of movement. Through the invention of his "photographic gun," he wanted to arrest the flight of a gull so as to be able to see in a fixed format every single successive freeze-frame of a continuous flow of flight, the mechanism of which had eluded all observers until his invention. What we need is the reverse: the problem with buildings is that they look desperately static. It seems almost impossible to grasp them as movement, as flight, as a series of transformations. Everybody knows—and especially architects, of course—that a building is not a static object but a moving *project*, and that even once it is has been built, it ages, it is transformed by its users, modified by all of what happens inside and outside, and that it will pass or be renovated, adulterated and transformed beyond recognition. We know this, but the problem is that we have no equivalent of Marey's photographic gun: when we picture a building, it is always as a fixed, stolid structure that is there in four colors in the glossy magazines that customers flip through in architects' waiting rooms. If Marey was so frustrated not to be able to picture in a successive series of freeze-frames the flight of a gull, how irritating it is for us not to be able to picture, as one continuous movement, the project

fig. 1

figs. 2, 3

B

2

flow that makes up a building. Marey had the visual input of his eyes
and was able to establish the physiology of flight only after he invented
an artificial device (the photographic gun); we too need an artificial
device (a theory in this case) in order to be able to transform the static view
of a building into one among many successive freeze-frames that could at
last document the continuous flow that a building always is.

It is probably the beauty and powerful attraction of perspective drawing that is responsible for this strange idea that a building is a static
structure. No one, of course, lives in Euclidian space; it would be impossible,
and adding the "fourth dimension," as people say—that is, time—does
not make this system of coordinates a better cradle for "housing,"
so to speak, our own complex movements. But when you draw a building in
the perspective space invented in the Renaissance (and made more mobile
but not radically different by computer assisted design), you begin to
believe that when dealing with static objects, Euclidian space is a realist
description. The static view of buildings is a professional hazard of
drawing them too well.

This should not be the case, since the 3D-CAD rendering of a project
is so utterly unrealistic. Where do you place the angry clients and their
sometimes conflicting demands? Where do you insert the legal and city
planning constraints? Where do you locate the budgeting and the different
budget options? Where do you put the logistics of the many successive
trades? Where do you situate the subtle evaluation of skilled versus
unskilled practitioners? Where do you archive the many successive models
that you had to modify so as to absorb the continuous demands of so
many conflicting stakeholders—users, communities of neighbors, preserva-
tionists, clients, representatives of the government and city authorities?

NETWORKS

Essay

3

Where do you incorporate the changing program specifics? You need only to think for one minute, before confessing that Euclidian space is the space in which buildings are *drawn* on paper but not the environment in which buildings are *built*—and even less the world in which they are *lived*. We are back to Marey's problem in reverse: everyone agrees that a dead gull cannot say very much about how it flies, and yet, before time lapse photography, the dead gull was the only gull whose flight could be studied; everyone agrees that the drawing (or the photography) of a building as an object does not say anything about the "flight" of a building as a project, and yet we always fall back on Euclidian space as the only way to "capture" what a building is—only to complain that too many dimensions are missing. To consider a building only as a static object would be like gazing endlessly at a gull, high in the sky, without being able ever

fig. 4   to capture how it moves.

It is well known that we live in a very different world than that of Euclidian space: phenomenologists (and psychologists of the Gibsonian school) have never tired of showing that there is an immense distance in the way an embodied mind experiences its surroundings from the "objective" shape that "material" objects are said to possess. They have tried to add to the "Galilean" bodies rolling through Euclidian space, "human" bodies ambling through a "lived" environment.[1] All this is very well, except it does nothing more than to reproduce, at the level of architecture, the usual split between subjective and objective dimensions that has always paralyzed architectural theory—not to mention the well known split it has introduced between the architectural and engineering professions

B

AN ANT'S VIEW OF ARCHITECTURE   *Latour, Yaneva*

4

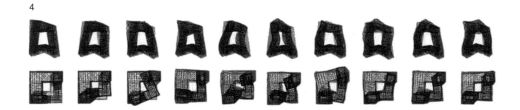

(and not to mention the catastrophic consequences it has had on philosophy proper). What is so strange in this argument is that it takes for granted that engineering drawings on a piece of paper and, later, projective geometry offer a good description of the so-called "material" world. This is the hidden presupposition in the whole of phenomenology: we have to add human subjective intentional dimensions to a "material" world that is well described by geometric shapes and mathematical calculations. The paradoxical aspect of this division of labor envisioned by those who want to add the "lived" dimensions of human perspective to the "objective" necessities of material existence is that, in order to avoid reducing humans to things, they first had to *reduce things to drawings*. It is not only the architects, his or her clients, de Certeau's pedestrians, Benjamin's *flaneurs* that do not live in Euclidian space—it is also the buildings themselves! If there is an injustice in "materializing" human embodied experience, there is an even greater injustice in reducing matter to what can be *drawn*. Matter is not "in" Euclidian space for the excellent reason that Euclidian space is our own way of accessing objects (of knowing and manipulating them) and making them move without transformation (that is, maintaining a certain number of characteristics); it is definitely *not* the way material entities (wood, steel, space, time, paint, marble, etc.) have to transform themselves to remain extant. Descartes's *res extensa* is not a metaphysical property of the world itself, but a highly specific, historically dated and technically limited way of drawing shapes on blank paper and adding shadows to them in a highly conventionalized way. To press the (admittedly philosophical) point further, it could be said that

I   Dalibor Vesely, *Architecture in the Age of Divided Representation: The Question of Creativity in the Shadow of Production* (Cambridge, MA: MIT Press, 2004). Steven Holl, Juhani Pallasmaa and Alberto Pérez-Gómez, *Questions of Perception: Phenomenology of Architecture* (San Francisco: William Stout, 2006).

NETWORKS

Essay

Euclidian space is a rather subjective, human-centered or at least knowl-edge-centered way of grasping entities, which does no justice to the ways humans *and things* get by in the world. If phenomenology may be praised for resisting the temptation to reduce humans to objects, it should be firmly condemned for not resisting the much stronger and much more damning temptation to reduce materiality to objectivity.

But what is even more extraordinary is that this famous Euclidian space, in which Galilean objects are supposed to roll like balls, is not even a good descriptor of the act of drawing a building. The best proof of this is the necessity for an architect, even at the very early moments of a project, to produce multiple models—sometimes physical models—and a great many different types of drawings in order to begin to grasp what he or she has in mind and how many different stakeholders can simultaneously be taken into account. Drawing and modeling do not constitute an immediate means of translation of the internal energies and fantasies of the architect's mind's eye, or a process of transferring ideas from a designer's mind into a physical form,[II] from a powerful "subjective" imagi-nation into various "material" expressions[III]. Rather, the hundreds of models and drawings produced in design form an artistically created primal matter that stimulates the haptic imagination,[IV] astonishes its creators instead of subserviently obeying them, and helps architects fix unfamiliar ideas, gain new knowledge about the building-to-come, and formulate new alternatives and "options," new unforeseen scenarios of realization. To follow the evolution of drawings in an architectural studio is like witnessing the successive exertions of a juggler who keeps adding more and more balls to his skilful acrobatic show. Every new technique of drawing and modeling serves to absorb a new difficulty and add it to the accu-mulation of elements necessary to entertain the possibility of building any-thing. It would be simply inappropriate to limit to *three dimensions* an activity that, by definition, means piling on more and more dimensions every time, so as eventually to "obtain" a plausible building, a building that stands. Every time a new constraint is to be taken into account—a zoning limit, a new fabric, a change in the financing scheme, a citizen's protest, a limit in the resistance of this or that material, a new popular fashion, a new client's concern, a new idea flowing into the studio—it is necessary to devise a new way to draw so as to capture this constraint and make it compatible with all the others.

B

AN ANT'S VIEW OF ARCHITECTURE *Latour, Yaneva*

So, during its flight, a building is never at rest and never in the shape of this Euclidian space that was supposed to be its "real material essence," to which one could then add its "symbolic," "human," "subjective," or "iconic" dimension. Very often models and drawings and the building stand side by side, and are amended and improved simultaneously. Under the pressure of construction, and in front of the eyes of astonished workers and engineers, architects constantly move back and forth between the building-in-construction and its numerous models and drawings, comparing, correcting and updating them. Architectural drawings, transformed into engineering blueprints and from there into the many pieces of paper used by the workers on site (glued to the walls, folded into attaché cases, smeared with coffee and paint) are still undergoing a bewildering number of transformations, none of them respecting the limits of what is described in only "three" dimensions... When a worker signs a drawing to prove that he or she has understood the workflow, is this in length, in height or in depth? When quasi-legal standards are added to the tolerance margins, which Euclidian dimension is this? The flow of transformations does not stop there, since once the building has been built, another problem of description arises: the building is now opaque to the eyes of those who are supposed to serve and maintain it. Here again you need completely new types of diagrams, new flow charts, new series of boards and labels, so as to archive and remember which part is where and how to access it in case of accident or the need for repair. So, at no time in the long succession of transformations through the cascade of many writing devices that accompany it during its flight, has a building ever been in Euclidian space. And yet we keep thinking of it as if its essence was that of a white cube translated without transformation through the *res extensa.*

What could possibly be the advantages of abandoning the static view of buildings in order to capture them (through a theoretical equivalent of Marey's photographic gun) as a flow of transformations? One advantage would, of course, be that the divide between the "subjective" and "objective" dimensions could be abandoned.

II   Tom Porter, *How Architects Visualize* (New York: Van Nostrand Reinhold, 1979).
III   Akiko Busch, *The Art of the Architectural Model* (New York: Design Press, 1991).

IV   Horst Bredekamp, "Frank Gehry and the Art of Drawing," in *Gehry Draws,* eds. Mark Rappolt and Robert Violette (Cambridge, MA: MIT Press, 2004), 11–29.

NETWORKS

Essay

The other would be that justice could at last be paid to the many
material dimensions of things (without limiting them in advance to the
epistemological straight jacket of 3D spatial manipulations.) Matter is
much too multidimensional, much too active, complex, surprising, and
counter-intuitive to be simply what is represented in the ghost-like rendering
of CAD screen shots.[V] Architectural design embraces a complex conglomer-
ate of many surprising agencies that are rarely taken into account by
architectural theory. As William James said, we material entities live in
a "pluriverse," not in a universe. Such accounts of design would reveal to
what extent architects are attached to non-humans such as physical
models, foam and cutters,[VI] renderings and computers[VII]. They can hardy
conceive a building without being assisted and amplified by the motor
potential of many thinking, drawing, or foam-cutting, hands. And that is what
makes them so materially interesting. Thus, the smallest inquiry into
architectural anthropology, the tiniest experiment with materials and shapes
shows to what extent an architect has to be equipped with diverse tools—
aids of imagination and instruments of thinking tied to the body—in
order to carry out the simplest procedure of visualizing a new building.
Another advantage would be that at last, humans' many various demands
could be fit into the *same optical space* as the building they are so
interested in. It is paradoxical to say that a building is always a "thing"
that is, etymologically, a contested gathering of many conflicting demands
and yet, having said that, to be utterly unable to *draw* those conflicting
claims in the same space as *what* they are conflicting about... Everyone
knows that a building is a contested territory and that it cannot be reduced
to what is and what it means, as architectural theory has traditionally
done.[VIII] Only by enlisting the movements of a building and accounting care-
fully for its "tribulations" would one be able to state its existence:
it would be equal to the building's extensive list of controversies and per-
formances over time, i.e. it would be equal to what it does, to the way
it resists attempts at transformation, allows certain visitors' actions and
impedes others, bugs observers, challenges city authorities, and mobilizes
different communities of actors. And yet we either see the uncontested
static object standing "out there," ready to be reinterpreted, or we
hear about the conflicting human purposes, but are never able to picture
the two together! Almost four centuries after perspective drawings and
more than two centuries after the invention of projective geometry

AN ANT'S VIEW OF ARCHITECTURE *Latour, Yaneva*

(by Gaspard Monge, a compatriot of Marey from the little Burgundian city
of Beaune!), there is still no convincing way to draw the controversial space
that a building almost always is. It is hard to believe that the powerful
visualizing tools we now possess are still unable to do more than Leonardo,
Dürer, or Piero.[IX] We should finally be able to picture a building as a
navigation through a controversial datascape: as an animated series of
projects, successful and failing, as a changing and criss-crossing trajectory of unstable definitions and expertise, of recalcitrant materials and
building technologies, of flip-flopping users' concerns and communities'
appraisals. That is, we should finally be able to picture a building as a moving
modulator regulating different intensities of engagement, redirecting
users' attention, mixing and putting people together, *concentrating* flows
of actors and *distributing* them so as to *compose* a productive force in
time-space. Rather than peacefully occupying a distinct analogical space,
a building-on-the-move leaves behind the spaces labeled and conceptual-
ized as enclosed, to navigate easily in open circuits. That is why as a
gull-in-a-flight in a complex and multiverse argumentative space, a building
appears to be composed of apertures and closures enabling, impeding
and even changing the speed of the free-floating actors, data and resources,
links and opinions, which are all in orbit, in a network, and never *within*
static enclosures (see the project MACOSPOL, www.macospol.eu and
www.designinaction.eu).

But one of the other advantages of taking a gull-in-flight view of
buildings would be that context could be done away with. "Context stinks,"
as Koolhaas so famously said. But it stinks only because it stays in
place too long and ends up rotting. Context would not stink so much if we
could see that it, too, moves along and flows just as buildings do. What
is a context in flight? It is made of the many dimensions that impinge at

V　Albena Yaneva, "How Buildings 'Surprise':
The Renovation of the *Alte Aula* in Vienna,"
*Science Studies: An Interdisciplinary Journal of
Science and Technology Studies*, special issue
"Understanding Architecture, Accounting Society,"
21(1), 2008 (in press).
VI　In the practice of Rem Koolhaas; see
Albena Yaneva, "Scaling Up and Down: Extraction
Trials in Architectural Design," *Social Studies
of Science* 35 (2005): 867–894.
VII　In the practices of Kengo Kuma; see Sophie
Houdart, "Des multiples manières d'être réel –

Les représentations en perspective dans le projet
d'architecture," *Terrain* 46 (2006): 107–122.
VIII　Juan Bonta, *Architecture and Its
Interpretation: A Study of Expressive Systems in
Architecture* (New York: Rizzoli, 1979). Charles
Jencks and George Baird, *Meaning in Architecture*
(London: Barrie & Rockliff, The Cresset Press,
1969). Robert Venturi and Denise Scott Brown,
Architecture as Signs and Systems (Cambridge, MA:
Belknap Press of Harvard University Press, 2004).
IX　Bruno Latour, "The Space of Contro-
versies," *New Geographies* 1, no. 1 (2008): 122–136.

NETWORKS

Essay

every stage on the development of a project: "context" is this little word that sums up all the various elements that have been bombarding the project from the beginning—fashions spread by critiques in architectural magazines, clichés that are burned into the minds of some clients, customs entrenched into zoning laws, types that have been taught in art and design schools by professors, visual habits that make neighbors rise against new visual habits in formation, etc. And of course, every new project modifies all the elements that try to contextualize it, and provokes contextual mutations, just like a Takamatsu machine.[x] In this sense, a building project resembles much more a complex ecology than it does a static object in Euclidian space. As many architects and architectural theorists have shown, biology offers much better metaphors for speaking about buildings.[xi]

As long as we have not found a way to do for buildings the reverse of what Marey managed to do for the flights of birds and the gaits of horses, architectural theory will be a rather parasitical endeavor that adds historical, philosophical, stylistic, and semiotic "dimensions" to a conception of buildings that has not moved an inch.[xii] That is, instead of analyzing the impact of Surrealism on the thinking and design philosophy of Rem Koolhaas, we should rather attempt to grasp the erratic behavior of the foam matter in the model-making venture in his office; instead of referring to the symbolism implicit in the architecture of the Richards Medical Research Laboratories in Pennsylvania as a scientific building, we should follow the painstaking ways its users reacted to and misused the building after the fact of its construction, and thus engaged in thorny negotiations with its architect Louis Kahn, with glass and daylight; instead of explaining the assembly building in Chandigarh with economic constraints or with the trivial conceptual repertoire of Le Corbusier's modernist style and his unique non-European experience in master planning, we should better witness the multifarious manifestations of recalcitrance of this building, resisting breezes, intense, sunlight and the microclimate of the Himalayas, etc. Only by generating *earthly* accounts of buildings and design processes, tracing pluralities of concrete entities in the specific spaces and times of their co-existence, instead of referring to abstract theoretical frameworks outside architecture, will architectural theory become a relevant field for architects, for end users, for promoters, and for builders. That is, a new task for architectural theory is coming to the fore: to find the equivalent of Marey's photographic gun and tackle

B

AN ANT'S VIEW OF ARCHITECTURE   *Latour, Yaneva*

the admittedly daunting task of inventing a visual vocabulary that will finally do justice to the "thingly" nature of buildings, by contrast to their tired, old "objective" nature.

X   Félix Guattari, "Les machines architectura-les de Shin Takamatsu" *Chimères* 21 (winter 1994): 127–141.
XI   Antoine Picon and Alessandra Ponte, *Architecture and the Sciences: Exchanging Metaphors* (New York: Princeton Architectural Press, 2003).
XII   Anthony Douglas King, *Buildings and Society: Essays on the Social Development of the Built Environment* (London: Routledge & Kegan Paul, 1980). Neil Leach, ed. *Rethinking Architecture* (London and New York: Routledge, 1997). Ian Borden and Jane Rendell, *Inter Sections: Architectural Histories and Critical Theories* (London and New York: Routledge, 2000).

THE ORACLE OF ATHENS: CONSTANTINOS DOXIADIS
AND THE STUDY OF HUMAN SETTLEMENTS

Jeannie Kim

Constantinos Doxiadis, born in 1913, was educated in
Athens and Berlin, and had entered the Greek government as a town planner when Italy attacked Greece in
1940. While fighting on the front as a scout for enemy
targets, Doxiadis founded an underground intelligence
organization that became the "scientific" general staff
of the resistance movement. At the same time, antici-
pating his post-war role, Doxiadis deployed his technicians to survey the damage and sketched out plans for
reconstruction, which he then published in his underground magazine, already entitled *Regional Planning
and Ekistics*. Immediately after the war ended, Doxiadis
opened an exhibition on reconstruction, easily convincing the Greek government that he should be in charge
of the country's rehabilitation. Doxiadis was sent to
San Francisco for the founding of the United Nations
and returned as the Minister for Reconstruction, a
position that he retained, despite repeated pressures
of a communist guerrilla war.

After an extended vacation in Australia on account
of his failing health, during which time Doxiadis became
a tomato farmer, he returned to Athens in 1953 to open
what was instantaneously the largest planning office
in Greece. Doxiadis Associates was housed in an eight-
story building adjacent to Doxiadis's own technical
university for the study of ekistics, and included a staff
of architects, planners, engineers, economists, soci-
ologists, geographers, and musicologists. Ekistics
sought to describe the matrix between five elements
(nature, anthropos, society, shells, networks) and five
forces (economic, social, political, technical, cultural)
that give each human settlement its own character. From
the Greek words for habitat (*ekos*) and settlement (*eko*),
the new science, ekistics, also consciously shared its
etymological root with "economics" and "ecology." The
tendency in ekistics towards taxonomy led to a clas-
sification of things at a global scale—laying the ground-
work for global planning through the research efforts
of the office, the teachings of the institute, and the
proselytizing of the journal.

Doxiadis managed to produce a global network of
acolytes through the sheer force of his charismatic
personality. This personality is evident in his self-pub-
lished books, which are often casual to the point of
sounding like self-help, with popular references and
frequent recourse to autobiography. He took a similar
approach to frequent press interviews and regularly
appeared on (mostly American) television with surprising ease. Similarly, his Delos cruises would place him in
contact with figures like Marshall McLuhan and Buckminster Fuller, the lambent setting of the Greek islands
seemingly erasing any potential for ideological friction.
The repeat participants of these symposia—Margaret
Mead, Arnold Toynbee, Charles Abrams, Edmund Bacon,
and Buckminster Fuller (who attended them all), among
others—would waver in their explicit support of Doxiadis's apparent agenda, but the conversations held on
the deck of the *Hellas* forged lifetime relationships and
chance encounters that made entire careers.

Through the combination of a school, an office, a
research institute, and a journal consisting largely of
material published elsewhere, Doxiadis brought people
and ideas together. The boundaries between these
various institutions were admittedly blurry and often
questioned, by financial backers like the Ford and Rock-
efeller Foundations, but also by foreign governments,
for example Pakistan. Because of these multiple efforts—and as a result of the work of indispensable
staff members like Jacqueline Tyrwhitt, who served as
the overqualified editor of *Ekistics*—Doxiadis was able
to establish and solidify his reputation despite a conspicuously diversified portfolio of interests and a pal-
pable sense of being spread too thin. The school would
eventually dissolve and the research institute would be
subsumed by the office, but *Ekistics* continues to be
both the touchstone of remaining Delians and the last
well of ekistic thought. Similarly, while the Delos symposia have ended, the notion of an alternate conference
where ideas are free continues to be rehearsed in offices, schools, and institutions around the world. Now,
as in the mid-20th century, the office continues to practice effortlessly in contexts that invite debate and
speculation about globalization and the ethics of development.

Doxiadis dreamt of global ecological balance, but
a planned balance. Bolstered by zero-laden figures,
Doxiadis Associates proceeded to tread fearlessly into
any country in need of planning and, significantly, "free
of the imperialist stigma." Given recent debates about
globalization and the continued effects of modernization upon the urban condition, the example of Doxiadis
can be of use in understanding the apparent failures
of the traditional disciplines of architecture, landscape,
and urban planning in the developing world.

BIBLIOGRAPHY
• Doxiadis, Constantinos A. *Ekistics: An Introduction
to the Science of Human Settlements*. New York: Oxford Uni-
versity Press, 1968.
• Kyrtsis, Alexandros-Andreas, ed. *Constantinos
A. Doxiadis: texts, design drawings, settlements*. Athens:
Ikaros, 2006.
• Pyla, Panayiota I. *Revisiting Scientific Epistemology in
Architecture: Ekistics and Modernism in the Middle East*.
Masters Thesis completed at the Massachusetts Institute of
Technology, 1994.

B   CONSTANTINOS DOXIADIS   *Jeannie Kim*

1   Doxiadis visiting the Applied Physics Laboratory at Johns Hopkins on February 7, 1969.
2   Image from a CBS radio interview and panel discussion following the presentation of the Greek delegation to the UN in San Francisco.

3   View from the desk of Doxiadis in the Athens office.
4   Doxiadis, Tange, their wives and an unidentified man during an excursion to the Japanese countryside, circa March 1967.

5   Doxiadis talking to a group of second-year Pakistani trainees of the Graduate School of Ekistics (GSE) on the premises of the Pakistan Institute of Ekistics (PIE) in Korangi, Pakistan, in March 1961.

1

2

4

5

MAS UD

Master of Advanced Studies in Urban Design
Eidgenössische Technische Hochschule Zürich (ETHZ)

Marc Angélil
Dawit Benti
Zegeye Cherenet
Sascha Delz
Kathrin Gimmel
Dirk Hebel
Darius Karácsony
Noboru Kawagishi
Bisrat Kifle
Tobias Klauser
Lukas Küng
Deane Simpson
Jörg Stollmann

URBAN TRANSFORMATION IN DEVELOPING TERRITORIES

Marc Angélil

Africa, the alleged "dark continent," and its patterns of urbanization processes are the focus of a design research program entitled Urban Transformation in Developing Territories. In a case study that considers Ethiopia, one of the poorest nations on earth, and its capital Addis Ababa, a form of projective investigation is promoted combining analysis, design, and implementation strategies—an inquiry directed toward practical performance.

Rather than upholding an *a priori* vision of an ideal city—one suggesting *tabula rasa* as a predominant practice—the transformation and gradual change of existing urban conditions is foregrounded. Following the saying that "Rome wasn't built in a day," the inquiry emphasizes the role of time-based techniques and process-oriented approaches. The urban fabric is understood not as a fixed entity in time but as a constantly evolving and adaptable system. Thus, design also entails the design of processes.

While research can use diagnostic techniques of analysis to trace the past evolution of urban systems in order to understand the *status quo*, it must also project and anticipate future developments. Accordingly, one of the key aspects of the work involves scenario planning: designing potential future conditions according to varying constraints. The long-term effect of changing parameters is tested and analyzed. Examples include shrinking and growing scenarios, the rate of developmental speed, questions of density, migration from rural to urban areas, changes in the demographic constitution of the social body, the allocation or lack of energy and monetary resources, the impact of forms of governance, etc.

Central to this undertaking are the transdisciplinary disposition of the work and the involvement of local stakeholders. A network of collaborators—including students, members of the academic community, professionals, governmental agencies, industry partners, and representatives of the public at large—frames the dialogue and negotiations pertaining to potential conversions of the built environment. These transformations are guided by the mandate to promote means for achieving socially, ecologically, and economically balanced urban settlements. The three-year project is structured according to three phases of investigation, each characterized by specific methods and conceptions of design research.

LEARNING FROM ADDIS (2007) builds on Robert Venturi and Denise Scott Brown's analysis of Las Vegas using mapping techniques as design tools to delineate both rereadings and rewritings of Addis Ababa's social and physical spaces.

ADDIS THROUGH THE LOOKING-GLASS (2008) explores, as in Lewis Carroll's Alice adventures, the possibilities of viewing the world from another vantage point in order to test design propositions as prototypical urban strategies in the different cultural contexts of Ethiopia and Switzerland.

QUO VADIS, ADDIS? (2009), with a nod to Henryk Sienkiewicz's political novel, seeks to generate design projects for implementation at the local level, and thus to counter prevalent tendencies to engulf Ethiopia in the global economic game.

Consider in this respect the mirror as a trope indexing different methods of design research. First, research might be regarded as an identity-forming device in the introspective, Lacanian sense: while looking at another culture, unexpected mirror-effects come into play; we see our own mirror image reflected in the very object of investigation. Second, research might be perceived as a type of mirror that entices us to penetrate its surface, to enter into another world, and from there to glimpse, through the mirror, the same familiarities of our own—a seemingly known world, though this time twisted, stretched, or magnified. Third, research might be looked at as a rearview mirror revealing players and events about to overtake us in the fast lane, in a type of *Back to the Future* setting—we know very well that "objects in the mirror are closer than they appear."

ADDIS THROUGH THE LOOKING-GLASS

Marc Angélil and Cary Siress

"There is the room you can see through the glass—
that's just the same as our drawing room, only the things go the other way."
—*Lewis Caroll*, Throught the Looking-Glass [i]

The back-and-forth of transactions, hustle and bustle of activities, hodgepodge assortment of goods, colors and smells are all simply breathtaking. Corrugated metal roofs cover stalls piled with diverse products offered for sale: woven baskets, coffee, charcoal, manure, used tires, building materials of every sort, and coffins made of wood. Thousands of people crowd the streets and alleys bartering along the way in the hope of making a good deal where possible. As the popular saying goes, "around here one can even bargain for a new soul." [ii]

This ostensibly simple spatial scheme is supported by a complex social network that ensures the performance of the overall urban system. The collective web is reinforced by craftsmen associations and trade unions housed in low-rise clusters, market halls, or, more recently, two- and three-story buildings. In turn, the neighborhood is zoned according to specific categories of services and products. For example, one encounters a sector for spices, another for agricultural produce, still others for light metalwork, textiles, plastics, and imported electronic equipment. Although the various subdivisions are ordered, the boundaries between them are blurred by the casual unfolding of events—or simply by the way things go, since the quasi-formal market organization is persistently thrown off balance by informal market practices.

With respect to the coexistence of formal and informal frameworks, the *Mercato* takes on the role of a key relay between rural and urban communities. It provides an arena for the sale of agricultural goods and serves as a landing pad for ever-increasing numbers of migrant farmers hoping to earn a better living in the city. As the majority of these migrants are not legally registered, they stand little chance of getting a commercial license. Nevertheless, their presence is tolerated. They occupy temporarily unclaimed spots wherever possible, peddling their products in the middle of the street, if necessary. Here, one encounters yet another level of land appropriation, this time in the form of a roaming proprietorship.

This machinery encompasses not only people who are on the move, but also the material resources of the city. Goods no longer used are salvaged and revalued for sale in the market—a type of recycling *avant la lettre*, a literal and opportunistic mining of the city that involves reprocessing whatever is at hand. That which in the West is typically considered waste—and thus worthless—is reappropriated in Addis Ababa through modest means and on-the-spot ingenuity: old tires are converted into satchels for pack-mules, soft drink bottles are turned into toys, and scrap metal is transformed into household utensils.[III] Other products, from discarded plastic sheets to recovered copper pipes, reinforcing bars, or beverage crates, need only be cleaned before being recirculated as building material. When the interplay of supply and demand is constrained by an economy of scarcity, there is no limit to improvisation. Bottom-up resourcing is the rule. When set into motion, such a principle gives rise to a self-fuelling system operating across multiple scales—a trickle-up urban ecology that reframes the discourse on sustainability.

I   Lewis Carroll, *Through the Looking-Glass,* first published 1872 (London: Penguin Books Ltd., 1998), 125–126.
II   Katrin Hildemann and Martin Fitzenreiter, *Äthiopien*

(Bielefeld: Peter Rump Publishers, 1999), 199.
III   Lukas Küng and Dirk Hebel, "Lernen von Addis Ababa," *archithese* (March/April 2007): 26, 31.

Despite dire conditions, such makeshift processing of resources gives rise to a special form of market economy, namely that of small-scale measures of subsistence carried out by the masses, organized from below, and empowered through the thousandfold repetition of minute elements. And yet, this frail economy recently faced a threat to its existence when the livelihood of local merchants and residents was directly confronted by the interests of a global consortium seeking a takeover of the quarter. What sparked the crisis was the offer of a Malaysian investment firm to buy all rights for use of the area, with the intention of turning the *Mercato* into a business and shopping district—an infringement from the outside hinting at a new form of domination. Followed scrupulously by the local press, the affair set off a public debate on the future development of the city. While politicians were occupied with the question of whether partaking in the global game would be either desirable or feasible, it was ultimately the cost of mass relocation that brought the entire venture to a grinding halt.[IV]

Two occurrence facilitated resolution of the conflict. First, the standoff reinforced social ties within the community and galvanized its political representation within the city at large. The worker associations were proactive in demanding an equal voice in shaping their environment, and new trade unions and building cooperatives were formed that further strengthened communal bonds. Second, at the time of the clash, the municipal administration was in the process of revising the existing zoning ordinance, the so-called *Addis Ababa Development Plan*. An entire chapter of building regulations was drafted for the *Mercato* area. To those responsible, it became clear that neither planning from the outside nor an exclusively top-down approach would serve the cause of appeasing the merchants and residents: their involvement in decision-making processes was paramount.[V]

What is referred to as "participatory" or "discursive" planning was legally ratified. Rather than succumbing to the demands of potential investors attempting to secure provisions for a high-rise business district, the city government sought consultation with citizens.[VI] Self-empowerment in place of dictated power became the maxim for all planning matters. Notable from the perspective of urban discourse is that the mandate in Addis Ababa to move from informal to formal structures is only possible under the condition of dialogue between public interests framed from above and those determined from below by the needs of the local population.

If we were to take another look in the mirror, another image of Africa would surface. Whereas the purported "dark continent" seemed ghostly to Michel Leiris in its sheer otherness and invisibility, as the title of his travel, log *Phantom Africa,* from the 1930s suggests, what appears phantasmal today is the strain of market economy that is engulfing the planet.[VII] Reflecting on the case of Addis Ababa shows us that what appears to be backward is actually a forward-looking tactic that can effectively circumvent the dictates of global capital through the implementation of communicative action in planning.

But just as any mirror can be shattered, so too can this fragile grassroots vision. A new form of colonization is well underway. For now, China, having spied lucrative trading prospects, has stepped through the window of opportunity. Putting the West ill at ease, an unexpected Sino-African dynamic is building, evoking memories of the European seizure of the continent. Notwithstanding complaints from Western companies that Chinese bids are impossible to match, the People's Republic has learned to play the game of coaxing African countries along the path of development. In marked contrast to Western investments that tie trade incentives to human rights, China's policy of "no-strings aid" is simply more seductive.

Ethiopia is not exempt from this lure. Here new infrastructures, schools, and factories are being built, favorable trading agreements signed, and vocational programs sponsored. On top of this, China recently gave a gift in the amount of 150 million US dollars for an annex to the African Union headquarters in Addis Ababa. But all of this comes at a price: substandard wages; no retirement benefits; no customs revenue from imports; no income from tax-free accords; and, above all, general disregard for the rights of citizens. Those browsing through the *Mercato* today would not be surprised to discover artifacts bearing the ubiquitous label "Made in China." In effect, exploitation is the name of the game. "Let's pretend" we in the West are out in front, looking back at the rest of the world.[VIII] But a second glance in the rearview mirror reveals another player about to overtake us in the fast lane. We would do well to recall that objects in the mirror are closer than they appear.

IV   The authors were informed of the unfolding of events in discussions with representatives from the Association of Ethiopian Architects in Addis Ababa in May 2007.

V   *Addis Ababa Development Plan*, 5, 43, 73, 74.

VI   See Jürgen Habermas's thesis pertaining to communicative action in *Theorie des kommunikativen Handelns* (Frankfurt: Suhrkamp Publishers, 1981).

VII   Michel Leiris, *L'Afrique fantôme* (1934), in *Michel Leiris. Miroir de l'Afrique,* ed. Jean Jamin (Paris: Quarto Gallimard 1996), 851, 855.

VIII   Lewis Carroll, *Through the Looking-Glass,* 124.

1   Africa as Alice's looking-glass, original illustration by *John Tenniel*, montage by *Charlotte Malterre-Barthes*

2   Italian master plan for Addis Ababa, circa 1939

3   Italian master plan for the relocated market quarter, circa 1939

1

2

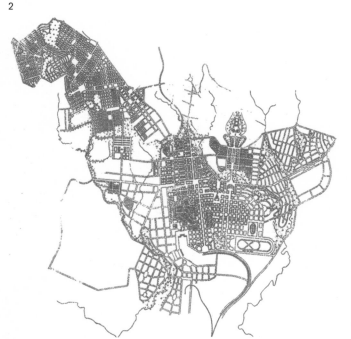

3

4   Main street in Mercato district,
photo by *Darius Karacsony*
5   Side alley in Mercato district,
photo by *Darius Karacsony*

6   New worker's cooperative in Mercato
district, photo by *Kathrin Gimmel*
7   Shipping containers integrated in
building facade, photo by *Lukas Kueng*

8   Proposed Chinese infrastructure
project for "Confusion Square," Addis Ababa
9   Chinese gift to the African Union,
Addis Ababa

4

5

6

7

8

9

LEARNING FROM ADDIS
The first design research studio of the postgraduate Master of Advanced Studies program Urban Transformation in Developing Territories (2007) examines the role of methods of analysis and mapping techniques as design tools to delineate both rereadings and rewritings of Addis Ababa's social and physical spaces. What can be learned from the case study and how can research spark design propositions? Avoiding the traps of exoticism and moral projections, the studio takes Addis Ababa's territorial organization and collective fabric as a model for understanding the forces at work in the formation of urban territories in developing countries—uncoordinated growth patterns, the lack of technical infrastructure, omnipresent poverty, migration from rural to urban regions, colliding financial interests, difficult negotiations between formal and informal processes, and complex social networks.

1   Colonial Africa 1935
2   Post-Colonial Africa
3   African Union since 9 September 1999

4   Topography, Ethiopia
5   Groundwater resources, Ethiopia
6   Conflicts Map, Ethiopia

7   Rivers and green spaces, Addis Ababa
8   Sub-cities and *kebeles*, Addis Ababa
9   Density: 4,000,000 inhabitants

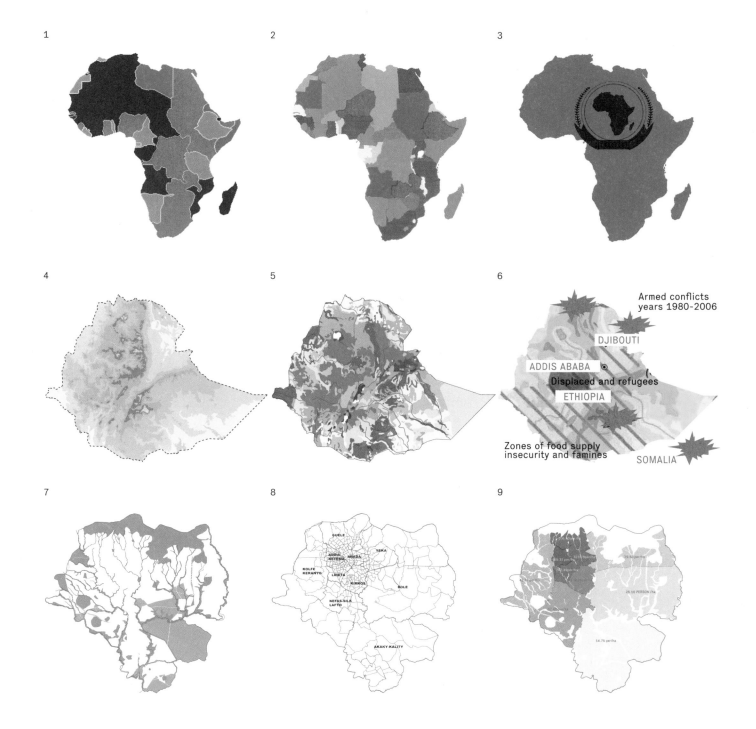

MIXCITY
Duan Fei, Kathrin Gimmel, Imke Mumm,
Stefanie Scherer

    1   COLLECTING—RECYCLING—RESELLING
Characteristic of Ethiopia's economy at both
macro and micro scales is the interaction of
formal and informal production processes.
A complex arrangement of activities is supported
by many involved groups: gatherers, craftsmen,
shopkeepers, traders, brokers, manufacturers,
etc. Of importance within this framework is the
collecting-recycling-reselling network centered
around the Mercato district. The collectors,
who come from rural regions, gather waste and
scrap material from all over the country, finance
their endeavors with loans from traders, and
sell their wares to wholesalers, who then resell
or recycle available products.

    2   SYNERGY URBANISM
Addis Ababa consists of a uniquely decentralized,
socially and programmatically mixed urban
fabric based on remarkable self-organizing
processes. Small-scale, informal economic
activities determine everyday life. Streets are
used for market purposes, the production of
goods, or religious and secular festivities.
Neighborhood organizations act as welfare and
community institutions. Different income groups
share the same districts. This amalgam of
participants, programs, and social frameworks
contributes to a specific spatial quality, one
marked by the interaction of multiple components
and diverse forces at work. Such a condition
suggests a type of "synergy urbanism" that
reinforces so-called social and programmatic
"mixity" in new developments, while maintaining
the hybrid urban properties of Addis Ababa.

    3   MIXCITY
The project intends to activate synergies on
different scales. Based on an analysis of
existing conditions, a catalog of rules and
multiple architectural prototypes is compiled.
Considering site-specific historical traces,
an urban strategy is identified that produces
"mixity" in every phase of development.

1

2

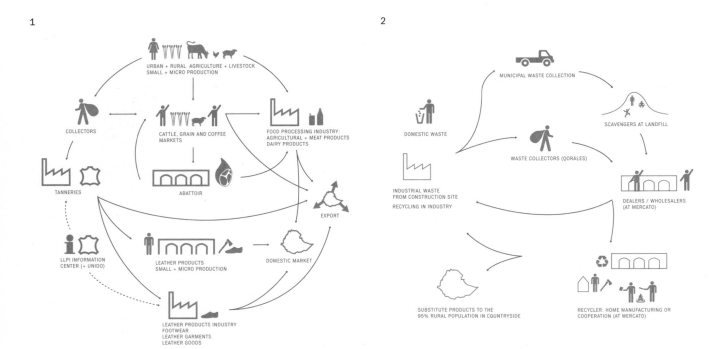

3

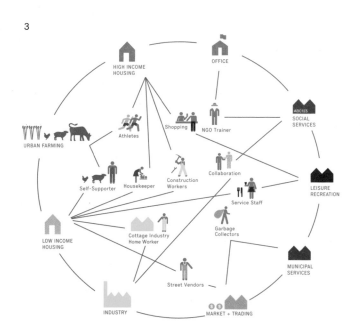

4   PLANNING GUIDELINES

The proposed guidelines, addressing equally formal and informal market forces, ensure that the diverse social fabric is maintained. A matrix of streets structures the neighborhood into distinct districts with identifiable qualities. The grid is further subdivided to define public spaces in both low- and high-end areas. 40% of any new project must be low-income housing to guarantee an appropriate mix. Additionally, slum-upgrading efforts must be undertaken in neighboring quarters, in collaboration with non-governmental organizations supporting the urban poor and their communities. To enhance programmatic synergies on the site, different functional clusters must overlap. Projected density regulations are adjusted to meet the needs of prospective users, such as low-density for low-income groups and high-density for the high-income population.

5   HYBRID PROTOTYPES

The proposed prototypes range from programming green open spaces to infrastructural networks and housing typologies targeting the involvement of a variety of participants. Those prototypes form the basic urban elements to be implemented depending on the programmatic and social mix of the individual urban sectors.

6   DEVELOPMENT PROCESS

To protect the overall organization of the site, a grid is implemented as soon as the land is available, creating fields of different width. Within these parcels, development can vary from self-built, temporary, to upgraded or permanent structures. This process is visualized in 5 possible scenarios.

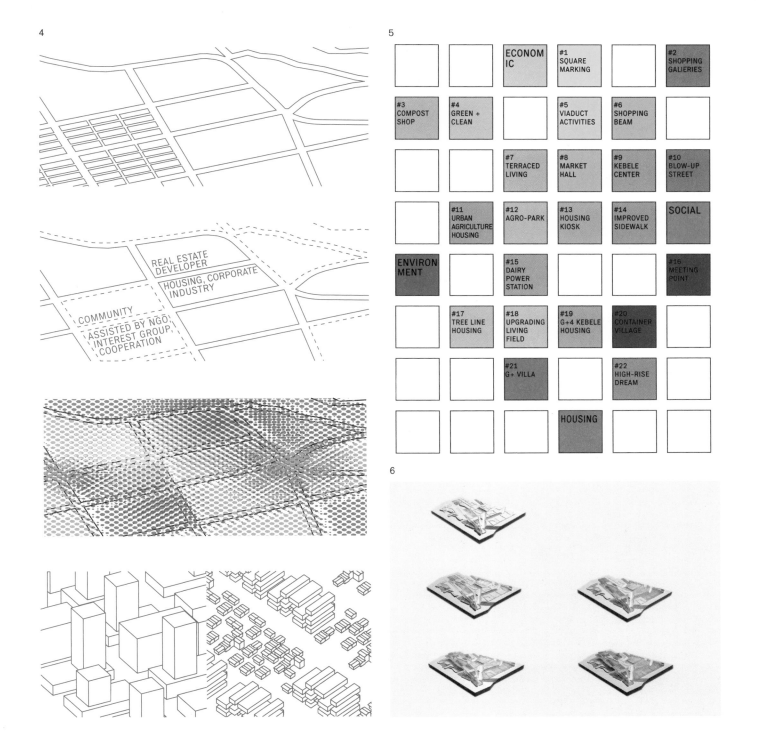

UNITE!
Charis Christodoulou, Hyeri Park

AIKIDO STRATEGY
The current real estate boom in Addis Ababa challenges existing low-income neighborhoods. The urban poor are the first to be displaced from the inner city to the outskirts in order to make the land accessible for more profitable developments. Accepting the fact that market forces are stronger than any potential resistance of the local population, the project suggests establishing synergies between market-driven densification supported by the

Local Development Plans (LDP) and inner-city slum upgrading processes. The LDP areas are currently exploited far beyond approved planning regulations, generating a high return for both the private and public sectors. The project proposes using this surplus profit to finance the step-by-step densification of adjacent slum areas.

1
a   Current situation of upgrading and LDP
b   UNITE, upgrading and LDP
c   actively, UNITE!, upgrading and LDP

2
a   roof material: corrugated iron
b   vertical open space
c   self-infill housing
     material: mainly brick
d   container informal housing
e   housing: for inhabitants
     (informal, self-infill) + selling to
     others (fully-furnished)
f   commercial: small offices and shops
g   street infill: according to the original
     street of existing informal housing
     or mall shops

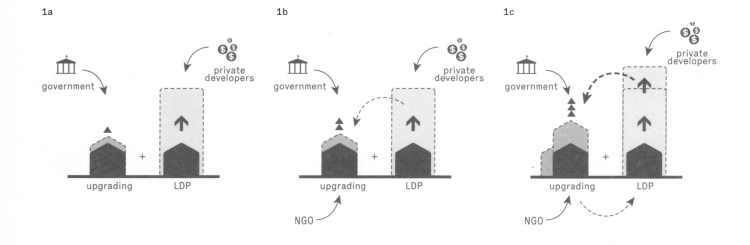

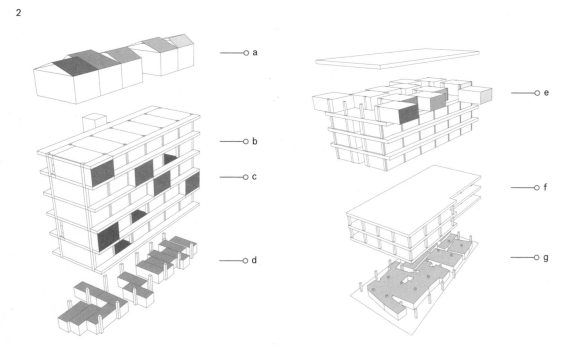

OLYMPIC CITY
Ann-Charlotte Malterre-Barthes,
Valentina Genini

ALIBI STRATEGY
The project Olympic City uses a design strategy based on a Trojan horse tactic. A long-term goal is proclaimed in order to achieve an otherwise impossible urban planning coordination. The project suggests sthat Addis Ababa could compete to become an Olympic City in the nearby future. As a virtual scenario, "Olympia"

becomes the catalyst for a series of upgrade initiatives related to national and international sport events—creating public open spaces and promoting infrastructure improvements for the city. According to a detailed timeline, the major sports events—such as the Great Ethiopian Run and the Pan-African Games—are evaluated in relation to potential urban propositions. This strategy derives its design principles from an understanding of existing political agendas and economic speculations—as irrational and absurd as they might be.

3   Olympic Diagram
4a   Before
4b   After
5   Proposed Marathon Route

3

UPGRADING THE CITY
IMMEDIATE GOAL

AN UPGRADED HOST CITY
FUTURE GOAL

SPORT FACILITIES

NECESSARY INFRASTRUCTURES

BASIC/PHYSIOLOGICAL NEEDS
★ ★ ★ ★

ABSTRACT NEEDS

Water supplies   Sanitation/Sewage   Housing (Safety)   Electricity Supplies   Health Services   Love/Esteem   Family

PRIMARY/SAFETY NEEDS
★ ★ ★

Transportation   Education   Social Services   Communication   Economy/Work   Friends   Justice

SECONDARY/SOCIAL NEEDS
★ ★

Media/Prevention   Society/Collectivity   Religion   Environment   Green/Public Epaces   Human Rights/Gender Equality

FURTHER DEVELOPMENT
★

Global Infrastructures   Ring Road   Tourism   Culture/Leisure   Railroad   Housing Programs

4a

4b

5

☆ Existing Festival Places
○ Existing Public Stadiums
● Proposed Stadiums
★ Proposed Festival Places
● Private/Minor Sport Venues

ADDIS THROUGH THE LOOKING-GLASS
The second phase (2008) in the sequence of three design research studios explores the potential of comparative analysis to test design propositions as prototypical urban strategies in the different cultural contexts of Ethiopia and Switzerland. The two case studies—Addis Ababa and the Schwyz Valley—could not be more dissimilar: one represents a rapidly growing metropolis in one of the poorest countries on the African continent and the other a rural agglomeration in one of the richest nations of the world. Questions relevant to both places are tested and transfers of concepts investigated, foregrounding similarities and differences. A mirror effect comes into play. Of significance for the research is not only the focus on physical products but also the interest in the design of processes. So-called toolboxes, comprising analytical, design, and communication instruments, are developed to help identify and structure future courses of action.

1a

1b

2a

AREA: 1,127,127 SQ KM

2b

AREA: 41,290 SQ KM

POPULATION: 78,254,090

POPULATION: 7,581,520

POPULATION GROWTH RATE: 2.231%

POPULATION GROWTH RATE: 0.329%

LIFE EXPECTANCY: 49.43 YEARS

LIFE EXPECTANCY: 80.74 YEARS

GDP PER CAPITA: USD 700

GDP PER CAPITA: USD 39,800

PUBLIC SPACE AS URBAN INFRASTRUCTURE

COMPARATIVE PROJECTING
A design proposition is concurrently tested in two fundamentally different contexts: Switzerland and Ethiopia. In spite of their differences, a discontinuous urban fabric and a lack of public spaces mark both sites. Taking this condition as a point of departure, the projects introduce a series of parks and open spaces within the existing urban terrain —a type of green infrastructure as a matrix to guide future developments.

ZENTRALPARK / CENTRAL PARK
Case Study Schwyz, Lukas Kueng

The Schwyz Valley, a compound of independent small municipalities at the fringes of the Zurich metropolitan region, has recently evolved into an urbanized landscape, displaying all the properties of a typical agglomeration—a terrain formed by a heterogeneous assembly of buildings, punctuated by agricultural fields, and crisscrossed by massive traffic infrastructure. Open spaces in-between offer a last glimpse of a rural countryside about to be replaced by scattered housing developments.

In order to generate a common ground that provides the basis for coordinated, inter-municipal urban planning, the project proposes a continuous park and network of open spaces for public use. The low-maintenance green spaces frame a type of landscape infrastructure, providing retention basins to prevent flooding, missing links between disconnected areas, alternative energy production sites, and sports facilities for the whole valley.
  1a   Temporary Lake
  1b   Densification of Former
Concrete Factory
  1c   Metropolitan Playground
  2   Brunnen, Switzerland

1a

1b

1c

2

NETWORK PARK—DECENTRALIZED PUBLIC SPACE
Tibebu Desta Daniel, Sander Laureys

Behind the official facade of Addis Ababa's city center with its large boulevards and monumental buildings is a dense fabric of single-storey informal housing, fully secluded inside the larger urban blocks. Beneath the city and all the more out of sight are the multiple rivers and creeks that traverse the capital from north to south. Part of the city's drainage system and mostly used as waste dumps, the contaminated canals are a major hazard to public health.

This project proposes a system of landscape connections along the existing waterways—an infrastructural framework with greenery, including pathways, sanitary and waste collection facilities, as well as spaces for public activities. The initial project phase introduces a path on top of a newly constructed sewage line. The path follows the river bank and connects areas of urban agriculture with the city's central market. Going beyond the mere provision of technical infrastructure, the project underscores the significance of public space as a means to foster social identity.

TOP-DOWN AND BOTTOM-UP
Both projects rely on top-down decision-making processes and on public institutions' ability to incorporate urban concepts into planning guidelines, such as the "Richtplan" in Switzerland and the "Structural Plan" in Ethiopia. Yet the proposals also necessitate community-based, bottom-up support: use and maintenance schemes require participation in collective matters at the local level.

3a   Uncovering, Filwoha
3b   Connecting, Meskel Square
3c   Extending, Peacock Park
4   Addis Ababa, Ethiopia

3a

3b

3c

4

3a   Uncovering—A new public space that highlights the founding place of Addis Ababa in a monumental manifestation of the hot water spring.

3b   Connecting—By creating a modest counterpoint to Meskel Square, the notion of the river network is brought to the existing public space. A connection is being created, first visual then physical. Meskel square becomes part of the network park along the river banks.

3d   Experiencing—A walkway along the river banks combined with the necessary infrastructure for the city. A pathway that is, at the same time, an experiencing of nature and water, and an element of maintenance for the city of Addis Ababa.

e   Extending—Considering self-initiated activities as a potential. A symbiosis of maintenance and control of public space with a self-organized, economical activity for the people.

UPGRADING COMMERCIAL ZONES
Lincoln Lewis, Simon Kramer Vrscaj

COMPARATIVE PROJECTING
The method tracks the development of specific design solutions in essentially different cultural contexts. Commercial zones in Switzerland and Ethiopia are analyzed and scenarios for their potential future development identified. Both urban probes and proposed projects focus on the relation between the private and public sectors, the interdependency of retail uses on the one hand and communal activities on the other. The case studies selected are a shopping center in the Zurich agglomeration and the market quarter of Addis Ababa—a mono-functional suburban mall vs. a multi-functional urban neighborhood.

MYTHEN CENTER
The Mythen Center in the Schwyz Valley is the most important shopping mall of the region, attracting local and regional customers. The proposed strategy aims at an integration of additional uses within the existing complex: production facilities, housing, a cultural center, and public spaces. Instead of replacing the existing and currently profitable urban fabric, the strategy is based on fill-ins and add-ons.

1a–c   Mythen Center, Schwyz

1a

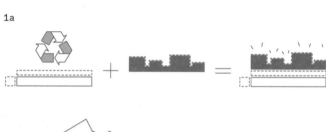

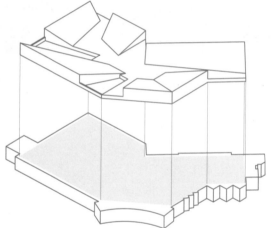

1b

1c

MERCATO
The project in the Mercato district of Addis Ababa suggests a series of upgrading measures strengthening community-based retail and protecting informal trade. Local associations of craftsmen and trade unions assert control over their neighborhood as an alternative to current proposals by global consortia, to develop the Mercato into a business and shopping area.

2   Overview of Mercato, Addis Ababa

3   Scales of Commerce in Addis Ababa
a   Associations
b   Formal
c   Informal/Illegal
4   Space Stuffers
5   Mercato, Addis Ababa

2

3

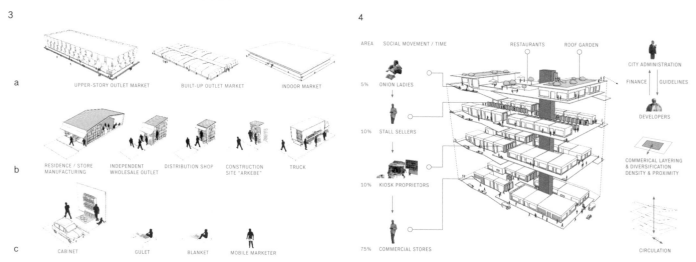

a   UPPER-STORY OUTLET MARKET   BUILT-UP OUTLET MARKET   INDOOR MARKET

b   RESIDENCE / STORE MANUFACTURING   INDEPENDENT WHOLESALE OUTLET   DISTRIBUTION SHOP   CONSTRUCTION SITE "ARKEBE"   TRUCK

c   CABINET   GULET   BLANKET   MOBILE MARKETER

4

AREA   SOCIAL MOVEMENT / TIME   RESTAURANTS   ROOF GARDEN

CITY ADMINISTRATION

5%   ONION LADIES

FINANCE | GUIDELINES

10%   STALL SELLERS

DEVELOPERS

10%   KIOSK PROPRIETORS

COMMERICAL LAYERING & DIVERSIFICATION DENSITY & PROXIMITY

75%   COMMERCIAL STORES

CIRCULATION

5

QUO VADIS, ADDIS?
Quo vadis, Addis (2009) focuses on the relation between research inquiry and practical performance. Reaching beyond academia, the approach strives to generate tangible design projects for potential implementation, working together with universities, aid organizations, governmental agencies, professional associations, and community representatives. Questioning ubiquitous tendencies to engulf Ethiopia in the global economic game, strategies are pursued to strengthen community-based projects that combine bottom-up and top-down approaches. The ambition is to promote future-oriented strategies in building construction, urban design, and territorial planning that implement new aptitudes in sustainable development. The work builds on a series of projects that are currently being developed by project partners, including proposals for new towns to counter migration, slum up-grading housing prototypes based on modular assemblies, and recycling strategies for new construction.

1   NEW ENERGY SELF-SUFFICIENT TOWN
Franz Oswald

NEST (<u>N</u>ew <u>E</u>nergy <u>S</u>elf-sufficient <u>T</u>own) is an initiative offering a proactive solution to the rapid expansion of Ethiopian cities due to population growth and migration from rural to urban regions. The project proposes a set of strategies for the development of new towns that can accommodate up to 10,000 inhabitants. Conceived as an adaptable system, the proposed scheme provides an urban matrix that can evolve and transform over time. Going beyond the construction of shelter, the undertaking aims at community-building. The core of the settlement, understood as a kind of town builder's center, includes a series of workshops and social amenities needed for both the formation and maintenance of a sustainable collective where inhabitants can learn, build, produce, or trade. The town provides its inhabitants sources of income, professional education, and communal institutions.

Of significance is the objective to create synergies through the coordinated deployment of renewable energy and material resources. Electrical power is locally generated by means of solar panels, windmills, or waterwheels. Waste management and recycling practices ensure the most effective use and reuse of basic materials and products. The project eventually seeks to achieve a highest possible degree of self-reliance through self-empowerment.

INITIATORS: *Martin Grunder, Surendra Kotecha, Corinne Kuenzli, Dieter Laepple, Franz Oswald, René Schaetti, Peter Schenker*

2   ADDIS-PREFAB
Sarah Graham and Marc Angélil

In order to alleviate the current housing shortage in Addis Ababa, approximately 50,000 new living units per year need to be built within the next decade. The Addis-Prefab project offers a concept for community-based development using a prefabricated housing system that can be integrated within existing settlements, avoiding eviction of the local population or relocation of entire neighborhoods into other urban areas. The proposal is conceived as a further measure in a series of programs conducted by the Addis Ababa City Government, the Environmental Development Office, and the Housing Development Project Office. The prefabricated units are to be constructed locally, building on current vocational training programs that encourage the formation of new businesses and micro-enterprises in the construction industry.

As existing structures within the slums are primarily single-storied, the project aims at a vertical densification of the urban fabric. Central to the concept is the provision of a basic structural matrix, including necessary sanitary equipment and partial enclosures, allowing users to continue construction and insert additional building components according to their needs—a do-it-yourself approach promoting identification and ownership.

3   UNITED_BOTTLE
Dirk Hebel and Jörg Stollmann with Tobias Klauser

United_Bottle proposes a new form of plastic bottle, designed to function as instant building material—operating with minimum means at the small scale, towards maximum impact at the large scale. The project's working hypothesis is that architectural work must go beyond the design of so-called final products and consider their life cycle processes. Learning from indigenous recycling practices in Addis Ababa, involving reprocessing whatever is at hand, the proposal investigates the potential use of PET and PP bottles as construction material for temporary and permanent structures in developing countries. Potential intersections of local material loops and global distribution circuits are explored through the secondary use of a product. Taking the increasing scarcity of resources into account, the proposition argues for the creation of surplus value through the introduction of additional recycling circuits.

Likewise, the water bottles can be deployed in crisis situations. Relief organizations and NGOs face two major challenges during a state of emergency: the distribution of potable water and the construction of emergency shelters. The project proposes to short-circuit cycles of mass-produced goods with those of crisis management to reduce both cargo weight and cost.

3

1

2

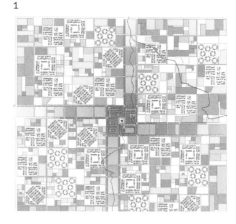

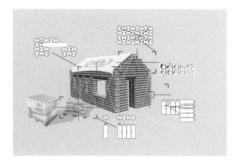

NETWORKS   Historical Case Study

A WEB OF RESEARCH ON SOCIO-PLASTICS:
TEAM 10 AND THE CRITICAL FRAMING OF EVERYDAY
URBAN ENVIRONMENTS

Tom Avermaete

A specific conception and methodology of research is beyond doubt one of the most characteristic features of the group of architects that gathered between 1953 and 1981 under the name of Team 10 and included, among others, Jaap Bakema and Aldo van Eyck from the Netherlands, Georges Candilis and Shadrach Woods from France, Giancarlo De Carlo from Italy, and Alison and Peter Smithson from the United Kingdom.

It can be argued that the very existence of Team 10 depended upon the confrontation of different research ventures. After all, it was at the 9th CIAM *(Congres Internationaux d'Architecture Moderne)* in 1953 that suddenly, teams of young architects refrained from presenting shiny modern urban projects that had yet to be built and rather showed detailed research of existing, dilapidated workers' neighborhoods. The so-called *Urban Re-Identification Grid* of Alison and Peter Smithson involved a photographic analysis of Bethnal Green in London, while the GAMMA architects *(Groupe d'Architectes Modernes Marocains)* such as Candilis and Woods presented research into the realities and rationales of the *bidonville* in Casablanca.

The Smithsons and the GAMMA architects were seriously challenging one of the most important research instruments of CIAM: the so-called CIAM Grille, or Grid. Introduced in 1947 by Le Corbusier, the Grid was composed of columns and rows of basic cells. The columns represented nine categories for analysis: milieu, land use, enclosed volume, equipment, ethics and aesthetics, economic and social influences, legislation, finance, and stages of realization. The rows corresponded to the four urban design themes around which CIAM had structured its thoughts since the first congresses: living, work, cultivation of body and spirit, and circulation. The CIAM Grid was a graphic means to present avant-garde urban projects in a unified fashion, with the two-fold intention of making different urban designs comparable as well as of defining universal design solutions.

Though the research subjects in the UR Grid and the GAMMA Grid were extremely different, the attitude was surprisingly similar. Both refrained from presenting an avant-garde design proposal, but rather reported a detailed investigation of the most ordinary neighborhoods in order to discover certain extraordinary qualities and more importantly to 'learn from' these environments about the relationship between built form and social practice. The Smithsons termed this relationship 'active socio-plastics.' The two grids elicited controversy among the participants of CIAM IX. Retrospectively, it seems that the reason for these vehement reactions was not the layout of the grids, which as Alison Smithson recalls, "virtually conformed to the standard 'Grille'," but rather their focus on the socio-plastics of everyday urban conditions.

The Team 10 group often attempted to engage with the complexities and nonlinear dynamics of the urban condition through association. This research goal resulted in a very specific research methodology based on associative thinking and represented by the figure of the collage, as the different panels of the UR and GAMMA Grids illustrate. Created with the liberal use of photocopy machines, silkscreen printing, cameras, and typewriting, the panels suggest a categorization that is based on human experience and imagination. The combination of a presentation of research and animated discussion that emerged at CIAM IX can be regarded as a declaration of the working method within Team 10. After 1953, this method of presenting hypotheses, studies, and research results to the inner circle of Team 10, as well as to other invited participants (including Louis Kahn, Fumiko Maki, and Kenzo Tange) would become the modus operandi.

Defining the identity of Team 10 has always been a difficult venture, as it was neither an organization of members nor a clear-cut movement. Rather, it was bound by an attitude toward research as confrontation and discussion, or as Alison Smithson recalls, "a working-together-technique where each pays attention to the other and to the whole."

BIBLIOGRAPHY
• Avermaete, Tom. *Another Modern: The Post-war Architecture and Urbanism of Candilis-Josic-Woods.* Rotterdam: NAi Publishers, 2005.
• Mumford, Eric. *The CIAM Discourse on Urbanism, 1928–1960.* Cambridge, MA: MIT Press, 2000.
• Risselada, Max and Dirk van den Heuvel. *Team 10: In Search of a Utopia of the Present.* Rotterdam: NAi Publishers, 2005.
• Smithson, Alison. *Team 10 Meetings.* New York: Rizzoli, 1991.

B TEAM 10 *Tom Avermaete*

1   Principles of the CIAM Grid, ASCORAL, 1948.
2   Panel from the Habitat du Plus Grand Nombre Grid, Groupe d'Architectes Modernes Marocains, CIAM IX, 1953.
3   Display principles of the CIAM Grid, ASCORAL, 1948.
4   Panels from the Urban Re-Identification Grid, Alison and Peter Smithson, CIAM IX, 1953.

1

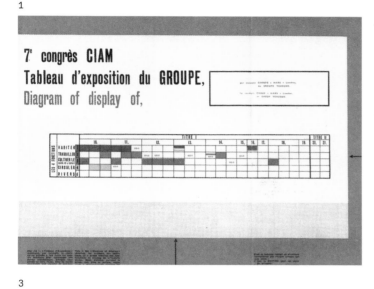

2

3

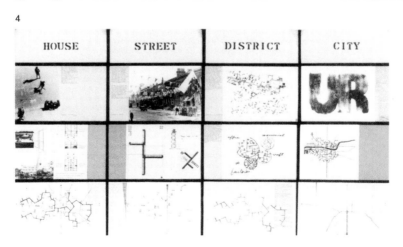

4

C

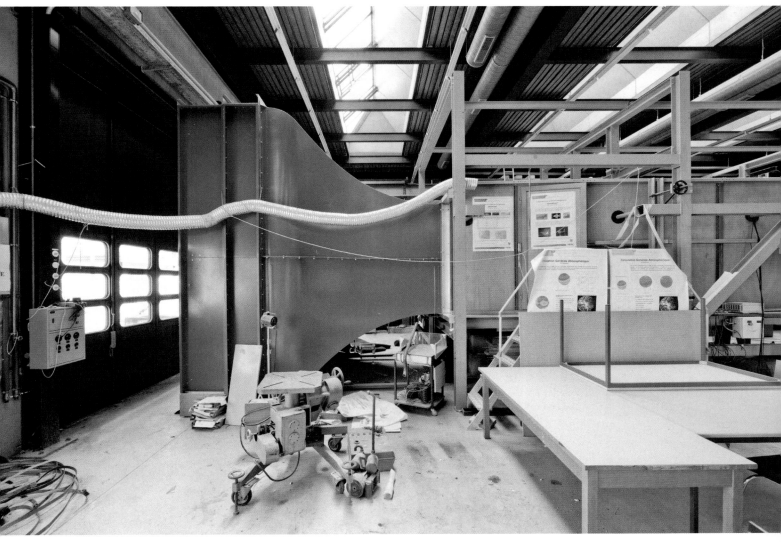

DIDACTICS

NOTES ON THE ANALYSIS OF FORM: CHRISTOPHER ALEXANDER AND THE LANGUAGE OF PATTERNS

Andri Gerber

Like many seminal figures of the 1960s, Christopher Alexander remains largely unconsidered today. This is not only due to our short historical memory; it is also closely tied to both his merits and shortcomings. While Alexander's work awakened great expectations in relation to design methodology, computational theory and system aesthetics, he never fully managed to fulfill them. Nevertheless, his rule-driven, generative process of design could well be considered an important antecedent of contemporary computational algorithmics and of emergence in architecture.

Alexander was born in Vienna and shortly thereafter was taken by his parents to England to escape the German annexation of Austria. As a young man at Cambridge, he first studied chemistry, then mathematics. Finally, he turned to architecture, but he found the lack of certitude in the discipline unsettling and felt himself forced to adopt a mimetic attitude towards what he supposed was required by the department. After Cambridge he was admitted to a newly created architectural PhD program at Harvard, where he wrote a thesis that was published as *Notes on the Synthesis of Form* in 1964. During the same period he also worked at the Massachusetts Institute of Technology (MIT). In 1963, he moved to Berkeley, where he is now Professor Emeritus.

The consequence of his mathematical training was a denunciation of the lack of coherence, the categorical arbitrariness and the amateurish approach to the complexity of post-industrial society characteristic of architecture. To counter this, Alexander sought to apply mathematical principles, in order to grasp a complexity that escapes the capacity of the human mind. Computation and mathematics served to decompose an architectural problem into manageable pieces that could then be recomposed into a project.

The main instrument for this process was the diagram, a tool he borrowed from science. Alexander differentiated between a form diagram, a requirements diagram, and a constitutive diagram, the third resulting from the first two. The diagram is an instrument that permits complex issues to be visualized and at the same time the synthesis of different sets to be proposed. Such diagrams express patterns, which are abstract structures of coherences between problems and solutions. Patterns are opposed to "things" or "objects" and produce a universal "pattern language," a hierarchical structure of differently scaled patterns, which everybody could use and "speak" to create coherent, and thus beautiful, forms. Ideally, patterns become invariants, perfect responses to the problems stated. Behind the idea of the pattern language also resides the desire to create a participative and democratic design process.

In 1967 he co-founded the Center for Environmental Structure at Berkeley, where he studied the possibilities for the application of his patterns in several projects. His teaching was likewise based on the development and application of such patterns on differently scaled projects.

However, many questions remained unanswered. Alexander started by considering *functional* problems; then he extended his attention to *aesthetic* and *morphological* problems, though never defining the nature of the problem itself. This fuzziness of the problem-statement has been the target of much criticism, mainly coming from the human sciences.

The second question concerns the nature of the composition of the generated sets: Alexander never managed to create a traceable process that would generate a resulting form out of these sets. Further, he abandoned the intention to deduce sets and patterns through computation, relying exclusively on what he considered a more immediate verbal description.

Paradoxically, the more banal the grounding of his design, the more complex his explanations became. Soon references to genetics and linguistics appeared in his writing.

At the end one could say that Alexander's work, lacking synthesis, was more of a "note on the *analysis of form*". Still, Alexander should be acknowledged for his application of computation in the process of decomposition—and this research should be considered in the context of parallel ongoing research such as that of Nicolas Negroponte at MIT and that of Lionel March at Cambridge—as well as for his work on diagrams. Interestingly enough, his "pattern language" influenced a whole branch of software development.

BIBLIOGRAPHY
• Alexander, Christopher. *Notes on the Synthesis of Form.* Cambridge: Harvard University Press, 1964.
• ——. *A Pattern Language: Towns, Buildings, Construction.* New York: Oxford University Press, 1977.
• Alexander, Christopher, et. al. *A New Theory of Urban Design.* New York: Oxford University Press, 1987.
• Alexander, Christopher, and Marvin L. Manheim. *Hidecs 2: A Computer Program for the Hierarchical Decomposition of a Set which has an Associated Linear Graph.* Department of Civil Engineering, MIT Publication No. 160, June 1962.
• Grabow, Stephen, and Christopher Alexander. *The Search for a New Paradigm in Architecture.* Stocksfield: Oriel Press, 1983.

C CHRISTOPHER ALEXANDER *Andri Gerber*

1a,b   Diagram explaining an increasingly complex design process

2a,b   Apparently chaotic content (2a)
comprehensibly rendered by means of
structuring in constellations (2b)

1a

1b

2a

2b

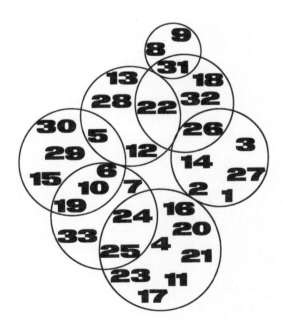

Essay

UNDERSTANDING BY DESIGN:
THE SYNTHETIC APPROACH TO INTELLIGENCE

Daniel Bisig, Rolf Pfeifer

Designing and building systems for selected abilities is a core activity of research in artificial intelligence. One of the attractive points of proceeding in this manner is that we not only end up with an actual system, but along the way, we learn a lot about its particular phenomenon, e.g. spontaneous structure formation or rapid locomotion. Our synthetic approach to intelligence promotes design and development as a research methodology. But in contrast to classical engineering, "understanding by design" promotes a bottom-up design trajectory based on "design for emergence."

"Understanding by design" is the name of a particular research methodology increasingly being employed in various sciences. This methodology forms the main foundation of embodied AI, as summarized in the textbook *Understanding Intelligence* [I] and the more popular *How the Body Shapes the Way We Think: A New View of Intelligence* [II].

Very briefly, understanding by design is based on the assumption that at least some natural phenomena can best be understood by building artifacts that embody a selected set of these properties. The process of building the artifact and its subsequent exposure to experimentation results in a tangible form of conceptualization and testable hypotheses. In addition, this approach leads to engineering innovations with general application potentials beyond the particular phenomenon under investigation.

The methodology of understanding by design combines two types of ideas, the synthetic approach and design for emergence. The synthetic approach introduces engineering practice into scientific research. Correspondingly, particular phenomena (e.g. recognizing a face in a crowd, or movement and walking) are approached from an implementation perspective. Design for emergence tries to minimize designer bias and the pre-definition of the artifact's resultant properties. This novel approach is uncommon both in engineering and science.

C

The term "synthetic method" was employed by psychologist Kenneth Craik to describe the process of testing behavioral theories through machine models.[III] The synthetic approach is not meant as a replacement but rather a complement for the traditional analytical approach. The analytical sciences are very well established and have immensely increased human knowledge about, and control over, the natural world. Nevertheless, starting around the second half of the twentieth century, science began to take notice of an increasing number of natural phenomena that seem notoriously to resist clarification. By now it is clear that these phenomena share some fundamental properties that largely defy an analytical approach. These phenomena are typically based on a large number of constituents operating in parallel and interacting with each other and their surroundings in a way that must be described by non-linear mathematical relationships. Also, we have become aware that these phenomena are not anomalies or exceptions, but rather represent the vast majority of systems. Examples abound in the purely physical world (e.g. climate, star formation, the creation of snowflakes), in biological organisms and societies (brains, gene regulation, body movement, swarm behavior, spread of diseases), as well as in man-made social, technical and socio-technical systems (cellular automata such as Conway's "Game of Life," the Internet, the stock market, cities, fashion trends). These phenomena are the result of the individual properties of the constituents (the neurons, the "cells" in a cellular automaton, or the humans in a fashion-trend network), and of the complex interaction patterns among these constituents. By building artifacts from the bottom up, from components to compound aggregates to whole systems, the synthetic sciences can study the properties of a whole system and how these properties depend on the interrelationships and behaviors of the system's components.

Design for emergence emphasizes the relationship between a system's high level and low level properties even more strongly than the synthetic methodology does. Emergence comes in different guises.[IV] [a] The behavior of an individual is always emergent in the sense that it is the result of the

I   Rolf Pfeifer and Christian Scheier, *Understanding Intelligence* (Cambridge, MA: MIT Press, 1999).

II   Rolf Pfeifer and Josh Bongard, *How the Body Shapes the Way We Think: A New View of Intelligence* (Cambridge, MA: MIT Press, 2007).

III   Kenneth J. W. Craik, *The Nature of Explanation* (Cambridge: Cambridge University Press, 1943).

IV   Pfeifer and Bongard, *How the Body Shapes the Way We Think*.

DIDACTICS

Essay

individual's interaction with the real world. Accordingly, behavior cannot be fully specified by some internal control mechanism but depends on the morphological, material, and environmental conditions as well. [b] An organism (or an artifact in engineering) is said to emerge from an evolutionary process. If this process follows principles of natural evolution, then all of the organism's capabilities are emergent properties of a process driven solely by the organism's reproductive success. [c] A collection of parts or a population of agents can display emergence based on local rules of interaction. For example, proteins assemble into a viral body architecture or a group of birds self-organizes into a flock. The overall behavior of such systems is not the sum of the individual behaviors of its constituent parts—it is entirely different, both quantitatively and qualitatively. For example, insect societies can build sophisticated hive structures despite the limited cognitive capabilities of each single insect. The fact that the human brain can exhibit consciousness is another impressive example. This capability is obviously not present in the brain's individual neurons.

It is impossible to define an analytic causality between local and global properties of an emergent system because they are mutually contingent upon each other: global structure and behaviors are the result of the interaction of the individual components, and the individual components are in turn influenced by the global behavioral patterns. It seems that many of the impressive capabilities of natural systems, such as their adaptivity, robustness, and capability for self-repair and reproduction, are the result of emergent processes. The implications of these insights for science and engineering can hardly be overestimated. In order for science to study principles of living and intelligent systems, it has to shift its focus (at least partially) away from the level at which these phenomena manifest themselves —the global behavior pattern—to lower levels (i.e. material and morphological properties and physical principles), even though, at first glance, these might seem unrelated to the topic of interest. Because the analytical treatment of emergent phenomena has proven very difficult, scientists have had to adopt an empirical position that relies on observation, experimentation, and trial and error. This means that in order to understand how changes in an emergent system affect its behavior, a scientist has to devise experimental setups and scenarios within which the system can evolve over time. Only within such a setup can the scientist test hypotheses about what a system's behavior depends on. For example, it can be tested how

C

UNDERSTANDING BY DESIGN *Bisig, Pfeifer*

the shape of a swarm or flock depends on the sensory capabilities of the individual agents, or it can be studied how the quality and diversity of evolutionary adaptations change in response to differing levels of selection pressure. For this type of experiment, a "trial and error" approach is justified by the fact that many of these relationships cannot be predicted, but are stumbled upon accidentally. "Trial and error" can serve as a strategy to sample a vast range of potential interdependencies. In addition, it helps to overcome a scientist's preconception and bias.

With regard to engineering, it is clear that many of the previously mentioned capabilities of natural systems, such as autonomy, robustness, and the ability to deal with unexpected situations, would be desirable for artificial systems as well (e.g. robots that interact with humans, vehicles for extraterrestrial exploration). Because of the principles of emergence, it is obviously difficult, if not impossible, to design such artifacts by following a classical engineering methodology (i.e. moving from the top down, from pre-specified high level requirements to low level implementation details). Furthermore, an engineer's expertise and intuition may not only be of very limited utility, but it might prove to be an obstacle in achieving the desired artifact properties. For example, methods from classical control engineering —while extremely efficient in a highly controlled industrial environment— do not work well when applied to building robots that have to deal with the real world. The real world changes dynamically and is only partly predictable, and agents within it have to act in the face of uncertainty. For this reason, the design for emergence approach also tries to minimize the human designer's bias and preconceptions. The usefulness and innovative potentials of this approach for engineering have already been proven. By applying design principles extracted from biology and exploiting ideas from natural evolution, with minimal human intervention artifacts have been created that surpass the capabilities of their human-designed counterparts.[V]

When designing systems within the context of the synthetic methodology, a scientist usually has to decide between a simulation- or robotics based implementation. Due to the fact that a purely simulation based approach usually benefits from lower costs and time investments, it might seem difficult to justify the development of robots. However, behavior as an emergent

V   John R. Koza, Martin A. Keane, Jessen Yu, Forrest H. Bennett, and William Mydlowec, "Automatic Creation of Human-Competitive Programs and Con- trollers by Means of Genetic Programming," *Genetic Programming and Evolvable Machines* 1 no. 1–2 (2000): 121–164.

Essay

phenomenon critically depends on physically realistic agent-environment interactions. It is very hard to achieve physically realistic behavior in simulation. The indefinite richness of the real world is the main driving force behind the diversity of morphologies and behaviors we witness in biological organisms, and a simulation possesses only those properties that have been consciously and deliberately added to it. Thus, any simulation based experiment is hampered by the absence of properties that have not been implemented and that might turn out to be crucial for the manifestation of an emergent phenomenon. With that said, it is clear that simulations remain an indispensable tool for scientific research. Experiments that involve a large number of interacting agents can usually be realized in simulation only. The same holds true for evolutionary runs that involve co-adaptations of morphology and control. For this reason, robotic and simulation based experimentation complement each other and will remain the two main methods in synthetic methodology.

Finally, it is important to note that the blending of methodologies from science and engineering has significantly expanded the explanatory power of the sciences. Traditionally, the natural sciences have been preoccupied with the study of naturally existing systems, whereas the synthetic sciences that capitalize on understanding by design have expanded their focus of inquiry. These sciences no longer develop artifacts as part of their research process in order to imitate natural systems. Quite the contrary: many of the resulting robots and simulations don't represent any organisms that exist in nature. For this reason, the synthetic sciences are no longer limited to studying natural systems. To paraphrase Christopher Langton, one of the founding fathers of the field of artificial life, the synthetic sciences not only study "life as it is" but also "life as it could be." Accordingly, the understanding by design approach allows scientists to gain a more profound understanding of the fundamental aspects of life and intelligence than would be possible if their research focus was limited to natural systems only. The understanding by design approach has combined the endeavors of natural science and engineering into a venture that aspires to elucidate the very meaning of being alive and intelligent. As such it has trespassed into the territory of philosophy.

UNDERSTANDING BY DESIGN *Bisig, Pfeifer*

1a

1b

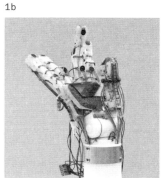

PROJECTS
The following projects aim to concretize the application of the understanding by design methodology in the context of embodied intelligence. These examples have been selected in order to highlight the methodology's impact for a broad range of projects and activities.

ROBOTIC HAND
The robotic hand project is used to investigate the relationship between morphology, intrinsic body dynamics, the generation of information structure through sensorimotor coordinated activity, and learning.[VI] The so called Yokoi hand is partially built from elastic, flexible and deformable materials. Its actuation is based on a muscle-tendon system inspired by the anatomy of the natural human hand. Furthermore, the robotic hand mimics some of the sensory capabilities of the biological original. Each finger is equipped with sensors for measuring bending, rotation and pressure. Additional pressure sensors are present on the hand's palm and back. In order to control

figs. 1a,b

VI   Gabriel Gómez, *Adaptive Learning Mechanisms for Autonomous Robots,* PhD Dissertation, Faculty of Mathematics and Science, University of Zurich, 2007. Gabriel Gómez, Alejandro Hernandez-Arieta, and Peter Eggenberger Hotz, *An Adaptive Neural Controller for a Tendon Driven Robotic Hand,* proceedings of the 9th International Conference on Intelligent Autonomous Systems (Tokyo: IOS Press, 2006), 298–307. Gabriel Gómez, Max Lungarella, and Danesh Tarapore. *Information-Theoretic Approach to Embodied Category Learning,* Proceedings of the 10th International Symposium on Artificial Life and Robotics, AROB 10 (Beppu, Japan, 2005) 332–337.

DIDACTICS

Essay

2a

2b

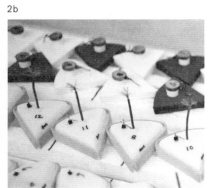

the robotic hand, biologically inspired learning mechanisms have been implemented. These mechanisms enable the hand to explore its own movement capabilities. By correlating the hand's sensory input to its motor outputs, it can also learn to manipulate and grasp objects. The robotic hand project has diversified its initial research focus and is currently moving toward application as a prosthetics device. For prosthetics, it is essential that the utilization of the hand "feel" natural. For grasping, an information structure must be induced, which implies that there must be rich sensory feedback. Experiments with fMRI show that patients provided with even minimal, but correlated, sensory feedback (such as electrical stimulation to the skin or mechanical vibration), integrate their prosthesis into their body schema much faster. [VII] This project illustrates that the synthetic methodology and the notions of morphology and information self-structuring benefit working systems and can give indications as to how to augment the sensory-motor "intelligence" of a coupled man-machine system.

ROBOTIC SELF-ASSEMBLY
The goal of this project is to achieve self-assembly and self-repair in a self-organized robotic system consisting of many modules. [VIII] Self-assembly is a process through which an organized structure spontaneously forms from simple parts. Despite the fact that this crucial process is ubiquitous in nature, little is known about its underlying mechanisms and not much effort has been devoted to abstracting higher level design principles. Taking inspiration from biological examples of self-assembly, we designed and built a series of modular robotic systems consisting of centimeter-sized autonomous plastic tiles capable of aggregation on the surface of

C

2c

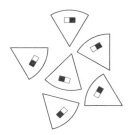 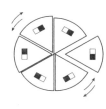 

figs. 2a–c   water. A single module, called a "tribolon," consists basically of a foamed rubber shape and a small vibrator. Power for the vibrator is provided via an antenna which touches the aluminum ceiling, connected to a power supply. Magnets attached to the modules let them attract or repel each other. The vibration causes the modules to move, and depending on the shape of the modules, different behaviors emerge, such as clustering and rotating. By drawing from our current experience in designing, constructing, and controlling macroscopic modular systems, we hope that we will be able to derive conclusions about the level of autonomy that is needed to achieve self-assembly. Our synthetic approach follows the biological principle that components self-construct themselves into organisms in a completely bottom-up fashion.

EDUCATIONAL ROBOTICS

The DREAM (Development of a Robot kit for Education, Art, and More) project aims at developing an educational robotics kit, consisting of hardware, software, and instructional material, which aids in communicating conceptual and methodological principles of embodied artificial intelligence to people within and outside the AI community. This kit is intended to promote creative and integrative approaches through a "constructionist" educational

VII   Alejandro Hernandez-Arieta, Konstantinos Dermitzakis, Dana Damian, Max Lungarella, and Rolf Pfeifer, "Sensory-Motor Coupling in Rehabilitation Robotics," *Service Robotics* (in press).

VIII   Shuhei Miyashita, Maik Hadorn, and Peter Eggenberger Hotz, "Self-Assemble of Water Floating Active Units," IEEE International Conference on Mechatronics (Harbin, 2007); Shuhei Miyashita, Marco Kessler and Max Lungarella, "How Morphology Affects Self-Assembly in a Stochastic Modular Robot," IEEE International Conference on Robotics and Automation, ICRA08 (Pasadena CA, 2008).

DIDACTICS

Essay

3

fig. 3

approach[IX] where students learn by developing and building artifacts.
The DREAM project builds on the AILab's numerous educational activities.
For example, we are participants in the Roberta network, which aims at
developing a robotics education program that specifically targets the interests of girls.[X] The AILab also teaches courses as part of the bugnplay.ch
art, media and technology competition, which is organized by MIGROS
Kulturprozent, and targets children from eleven to twenty years old. These
activities are based on our conviction that the concepts of embodied AI
research are not only relevant to the scientific community within this specific field but have far-reaching implications for scientific research and
engineering in general. Furthermore, we have observed that the synthetic
methodology is well suited in an education context, in that it helps to
inspire and maintain a high level of motivation in students and can communicate even very abstract concepts in a comprehensible and tangible
way.[XI] Contrary to existing educational robotics kits, the DREAM kit
intends to promote principles and methodologies from embodied AI research
that are central to the understanding by design approach. Accordingly,
the kit will emphasize bottom-up engineering and design for emergence.
We believe that these concepts encourage the search for new problem
solving strategies and are useful and inspiring for anybody who is
involved in problem solving and decision making in our highly dynamic,
complex, and only partially predictable world.

ROBOTIC ART INSTALLATION

The project HairMotion is an ongoing collaboration between one of the
authors and artist Valerie Bugmann. The project aims to realize an interactive
installation that serves as an experimental environment for non-verbal
communication. The robots are stationary and their only means of expression

C

UNDERSTANDING BY DESIGN   *Bisig, Pfeifer*

4a

4b

figs. 4a,b

is via the breathing movements of their artificial lungs and their pneumatically actuated hair. Set up in a circle, facing towards an inner space that can be entered by a visitor, the robots are capable of perceiving the presence and movements of the visitor within this space via a vision based tracking system. The robots' degree of autonomy and reactivity changes, and correspondingly the movements of the visitor and robots transition through periods of synchronization, correlation and independence. The scenario encourages visitors to engage the robots in a dialogue of movements in order to identify recurring elements of interaction. Accordingly, the installation creates an experimentation space that allows visitors to create and test syntactic and semantic features of a movement based, nonverbal language.

IX   Mitchel Resnick, "Distributed Constructionism," Proceedings of the International Conference of the Learning Sciences (Evanston IL: Northwestern University, 1996), 280–284.

X   Monika Müllerburg, Ulrike Petersen and Gabi Theidig, "Roboter in Bildung uns Ausbildung," in *FINUT-28. Kongress von Frauen in Naturwissenschaft und Technik*, ed. M. Calm (Darmstadt: FIT-Verlag, 2002)

227–234; Ulrike Petersen, Monika Müllerburg and Gabi Theidig, "Girls and Robots: A Promising Alliance" *ERCIM News* 53 (April 2003): 32–33.

XI   Chandana Paul, Verena Hafner and Josh C. Bongard, *Teaching New Artificial Intelligence using Constructionist Edutainment Robots*, GMD Workshop on Edutainment Robots (Sankt Augustin, Germany, 2000).

THE CITY AS ARCHITECTURE: ALDO ROSSI'S
DIDACTIC LEGACY

Filip Geerts

The legacy of Aldo Rossi is divided between two books, *The Architecture of the City* and *A Scientific Autobiography*, both seminal contributions to the disciplinary corpus of architecture. Originally published as *L'Architettura della città* in 1966 and since translated into many languages, the first is a standard feature on architecture school reading lists and seems to have become the kind of open text that is interpreted in various ways. It is commonly misunderstood, especially outside Italy, as simply a manual that instructs architects with regard to the historical context and typo-morphological analysis of the city. Instead the text can best be considered a treatise, because it defines the city (also) as architecture —as opposed to a phenomenon that is mainly of interest to sociology, anthropology, psychology, economics, history, or geography. Rossi evaluates other disciplines that deal with the city not in order to dismiss them, but to absorb them into a more holistic reading of the city as architecture. He makes an important and profoundly didactic step by translating what is relevant in these other disciplinary readings toward an architectural understanding of the city. By doing so he defines a self-determined autonomy of architecture, based not on (pseudo-) empirical neutrality waiting to be applied, but on tendency and choice. The treatise is characterized by what is now recognized as a "Rossian" desire to construct a theory, and to make it teachable. *A Scientific Autobiography*, initially published in English in 1981, is coincident with the rise of Rossi's star in the firmament of international architecture. This memoir, which is based on his 1970s notebooks and describes influences, obsessions, and fears together with his projects, is of course very different from the 1966 book. Nevertheless, it remains committed to installing rationality and resisting idiosyncrasy and contingency while asserting the centrality of the individual project—the artifact. Therefore the two books are not necessarily opposing statements. *A Scientific Autobiography* brings the self-determined autonomy of architecture into the realm of Rossi's own architectural work, one consequence of his theory made evident.

The Architecture of the City does not speak of the appropriateness of a certain architectural language, does not put typo-morphological analysis forward as a goal in itself, and is not a one-sided dismissal of the *città-regione* debate (i.e. the radical speculation surrounding the expanded and accelerated urban development in the early sixties in Italy). At the same time, however, it is also not a neutral canvas for whatever autonomous architectural experiment comes next, despite the fact that some of his now famous pupils from the 1970s in Zurich welcomed his reintroduction of architecture *an sich*. When receiving the 2001 Pritzker Prize together with Pierre de Meuron, Jacques Herzog said, "[Rossi] opened up many new horizons for us. Prior to his arrival, our first teacher was Lucius Burckhardt, who taught us that whatever we do, we should not build; instead we should think, we should learn about people. It was inspiring, but it was also frustrating. When Rossi came, he told us just the opposite. He said to forget sociology, return to architecture. [...] And we loved his writing, 'architecture is architecture' because it seems so provocatively simple-minded, and pinpoints something that is still vital to us today. Architecture can only survive as architecture in its physical and central diversity and not as a vehicle for an ideology of some kind."

This preference for the anti-ideological "architecture of the city" should not be mistaken for an absence of theory. All theory consists of a precise construction of what the "material" of architecture is, should, or could be, a concern shared by Rossi's contemporaries Grassi and Gregotti. *The Architecture of the City* achieved lasting relevance in part by making it possible to posit architecture again as an essential lens through which to see the city and the territory, without losing sight of the individuality of the architectural project. Gregotti's *Il Territorio dell'architettura*, also published in 1966, expresses a desire for a theory on the material of architecture by addressing more explicitly the territorial dimension, a concern that Rossi shared, though he left it open as a question—having experienced the often un-architectural *città-territorio* discussions of the early sixties. Grassi considers the question Rossi only answered later in his built work and to a lesser extent in his *Scientific Autobiography*: namely the precise relationship of the city-as-architecture to the individual project. Grassi's *La Costruzione logica dell'architettura* (1967) radically transcends the desire for theory by continuing instead the tradition of the manual—and by doing so, the timeless architectural practice as *mestiere* in the city. Early on in life, Grassi legitimized his "choice," his architecture—one already made by architects before him. Rossi kept on looking.

BIBLIOGRAPHY
• Lampugnani, Vittorio Magnago. "Die Architektur der Stadt als poetische Wissenschaft." In Aldo Rossi et al. *Die Suche nach dem Glück. Frühe Zeichnungen und Entwürfe.* 48–55. München: Prestel, 2003.
• Rossi, Aldo. *The Architecture of the City.* Cambridge MA: MIT Press, 1981.
• ——. *A Scientific Autobiography.* Cambridge MA: MIT Press, 1981.

C   ALDO ROSSI   *Filip Geerts*

1   Aldo Rossi, *La Città Analoga*, 1976, 102 × 100 cm, Private collection. Courtesy Fondazione Aldo Rossi © Eredi Aldo Rossi. From the concept postulated in *The Architecture of the City*, Rossi hypothesized "the analogous city" for the 1976 Venice Biennale, "… based on certain fundamental artifacts in the urban reality around which other artifacts are constituted within the framework of an analogous system … in which the elements were pre-established and formally defined, but where the significance that sprung forth at the end of the operation was the authentic, unforeseen, and original meaning of the work." (from the preface to the second Italian edition of *L'Architettura della città*, 1970) Panel by Aldo Rossi, Fabio Reinhart, Bruno Reichlin and Eraldo Consolascio for the 1976 Venice Architecture Biennale.

1

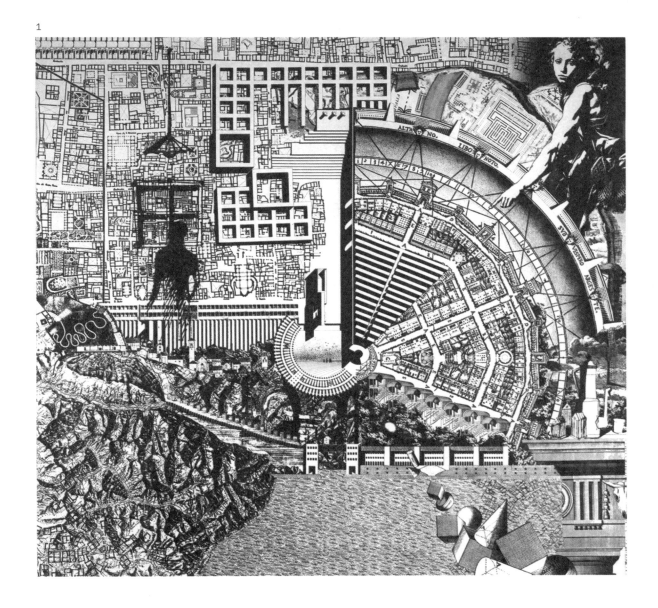

ALICE

Atelier de la conception de l'espace
Ecole Polytechnique Fédérale de Lausanne (EPFL)

Dieter Dietz
Aline Dubach
Eveline Galatis
Olivier Ottevaere
Isabella Pasqualini
Daniel Pokora
Katia Ritz
Marc Schmit

EXPLORING UNCOMMON TERRITORIES:
A SYNTHETIC APPROACH TO TEACHING ARCHITECTURE

Dieter Dietz

"My NAME is Alice, but—"
"It's a stupid enough name!" Humpty Dumpty interrupted impatiently.
"What does it mean?"
"MUST a name mean something?" Alice asked doubtfully.
"Of course it must," Humpty Dumpty said with a short laugh:
"MY name means the shape I am—and a good handsome shape it is, too.
With a name like yours, you might be any shape, almost."
—Lewis Carroll, Through the Looking Glass

RÉALITÉS PARALLÈLES

In its approach to teaching, ALICE explores uncommon territories. The choices of topics and sites purposefully combine the familiar with very particular geographical, economical or morphological circumstances. We emphasize working concurrently with multiple tools, such as physical models, 3-D software, images, 2-D programs, computer aided manufacturing, etc. ALICE modifies its curriculum each year to encompass new material and domains.

The idea of a parallel approach to the conception and production of architectural design is a central aspect of the didactic structure. All projects are literally developed both in the digital as well as in the physical world. With "Réalités parallèles" (parallel realities) we propose a method of intense engagement with the idea of making, not only in a physical sense—as in the crafting of models, drawings, or hand-drawn sketches—but also in a virtual sense, as in the production of digital models, visuals, databases, images, etc. The design process is constantly challenged by catalyst reactions in the respective fields of production.

In recent times, the size of our geophysical earth, the "physically far," has constantly been challenged by the "technologically near." Our planet has shrunk and continues to shrink into a comprehended object. Our experience of journey, both physical and mental, is being unintentionally eradicated by the loss of intervals and temporalities. On the other hand, this presents us with a fresh vantage point that we cannot occupy directly: the agravitational horizontal window relentlessly scanning the earth's surface: humankind's third eye.

How can architecture not only engage with, but possibly create resistance to this new frictionless world, using the available new technologies? Can architecture still perform as a conductor of flows, while working against the grain of the ever smoother, the ever faster—while remembering that the earth pulls us?

THE DESIGNER WITHIN

One of the key ideas underlying our design approach is the constant discourse between the conceptual framework of an architectural idea and its translation into an actual project. In an educational context at the bachelor level this involves on the one hand the articulation of an architecture project as a proposal represented in models and drawings, and on the other hand the development of a coherent program according to this architectural idea. While projects are usually developed with typical architectural drawings and models to represent a given proposal, we are presently exploring the potential of expanding the project scale into a one-to-one condition. The intention is that the structural constraints present at this scale as well as the potential physical and spatial impact will encourage synthetic thinking and a holistic approach to design issues.

In the academic year 2007/2008 a series of explorations of gravity formed the beginning of the semester. The students first produced a physical construct declaring gravity at work. This initial artifact was then subjected to a process of analysis, reevaluation and reinterpretation in 3-D software, physical models and architectural drawings, and was finally transformed into a proposal for a site-interactive installation or "pavilion" for the London Festival of Architecture held in June 2008. At the end of the first semester these proposals were entered in an internal, juried competition, resulting in a team of twelve students who would further develop the design and bring it to completion.

To realize construction of a pavilion or installation in a remote city with a second year design class is an experiment. The basic idea behind it is to expose students to processes in architectural production, from conception, to planning, to realization, to the ultimate removal of the architectural artifact—thus, the full life cycle of an object.

At the same time, such a project calls into question the position and the viewpoint of the designer. Here, the architect is not just a creator, he is also a craftsman, a producer, an engineer, a manager, etc. Thus the designer is not only acting from without or above—from a top-view position or a bird's-eye perspective —but also from within. The employment of different digital and physical tools, in addition to the actual building of a one-to-one structure, both presents multiple reference frames for the maker of the design, and also transgresses these frames. This altered position of the designer-architect implies understanding architectural design as an emergent process.

A SYNTHETIC APPROACH

This "synthetic" approach relates to the core concepts of "learning by building" and "embodiment" as they are employed in current research on artificial intelligence. In their recent book *How the Body Shapes the Way We Think,* Rolf Pfeifer and Josh Bongard argue that, in contrast to a view of intelligence as "control and computation," we cannot understand intelligence without building physical agents (robots) that are able to interact with the real world.

In our studio we employ a "messy" method that entails constantly making things on the foundations of formerly conceived ideas, and bringing them into a test-condition in physical reality. This testing will feed back directly into the realm of the project's ideas. The constant process of conceiving and testing is recorded in project-based sourcebooks, compilations of "archive copies" of images and reference material in chronological and indexed order. Thus, the ongoing process can be accessed or revisited at any time, by the student designer-makers or anyone visiting the ALICE website.

By expanding our project scales towards life size, we are now exploring the possibilities of "learning by building" in a one-to-one framework. While physical models can be seen as mediating tools between the abstract and the real, allowing for visual/physical simulations of spatial ideas and concepts, the one-to-one scale directly employs the human body as an interactive component of spatial exploration. The structures built at one to one are spatial agents and become part of our physical environment.

ALICE's main focus is space, as suggested by the name to which its acronym refers. Though a seemingly common property of architecture, the notion and concept of space are rarely addressed directly. Other aspects, such as tectonics, structure, materiality, as well as function, economics or further subtexts, tend to dominate architectural discourse, and space is often left as a residue of the many tasks that architecture is asked to perform.

It is our goal to explore the possibilities for reestablishing space as a flexible and powerful criterion in the discourse of environmental, urban, and architectural planning. The initial assumption is therefore that space in itself is not neutral or merely present.

This is a starting point of relevance for the consequences of constantly changing environmental conditions affecting the built space: a growing world population and subsequent urbanization; increased mobility and intensified supply chains; far stretched boundaries of the perceivable world through evolv-ing cultures; any of these matters affect the conditions of physical space and infer a constraining interaction between the urbanized and the non-inhabitable space on our everyday life.

In light of the revolutionary attitude of human projections on the environment throughout history, there is a clear need for any non-deterministic design methodologies that assimilate hypothetical knowledge and data analysis at the same level through a synthetic design approach. Therefore our design research examines the tools that are necessary to establish the link between different spatial frames at the interstices of the natural environment and its artificial surrounding.

PROCESSUAL KNOWLEDGE IN ARCHITECTURAL EDUCATION

Education is based on, incorporated as and processed by knowledge. To focus on knowledge as an event in process bypasses the dangers of a one-sided empirical or rationalist approach to knowledge as pure database. Instead, it embeds the process of design within the field of research itself.

We are interested in this shift of focus from knowledge as database towards knowledge as process, because it implies a substantial change in the structure of learning/teaching itself, a shift from making as reproducing towards making as reflecting the made in an ongoing process. Goals cannot then be described as determinate entities but are a "process towards" or a "way to." They are in permanent need of adjustment. This also partially implies that the search for predefined solutions is losing currency, while architectural instruments such as type and program remain tools (or parts of a language) that need constant reevaluation.

While design activities employ the methods and implements from domains adjacent to architecture—and therefore collaboration with experts in those fields is of great benefit—architecture also has the unique potential to explore knowledge processes as spatial events.

In grasping spatial aspects of knowledge processes and transforming them into a visual form or a spatial construction, this process of interpretation itself becomes a process of knowledge. Ultimately, the aesthetic reevaluation of a process becomes a project: scientific and architectural at the same time.

1

GRAVITY AT WORK
The first phase in the ALICE curriculum includes the fabrication of a "physical construct" based on explorations conducted through experiments. The physical construct is intended to "declare gravity at work."
1   Experiment with smoke and a cardboard grid in order to understand how the resistance of air affects the way a given structure falls.
Malaica Cimenti, Lila Held

2   Emphasis was given to the observation both of falling objects as well as the receiving ground. Here gravity is replaced through a vacuum forming device: the result suggests a gravitational force through its visual narrative.
Nicolas De Courten, Christopher Tan

3   The gravitational impact on falling object and receiving ground was observed as spatial and formal conditions manifested in compressed moments of time.
Andreas Gubler, Sandro Tonietti

2

3

DRAWING IN TIME
3-D software is implemented as a tool for analysis of spatial conditions and transformations in time. The parallel construction of a physical model and its counterpart in the digital realm fosters an understanding of structures and forces.

This project investigates how, with an increasing upward force, an initial two dimensional lattice redistributes itself into three dimensional space with some local attachments.
Nicolas De Courten, Christopher Tan

1,2   3-D CAD sequence drawing mapping deformation in time
3   Physical model, wood and elastic strings

2

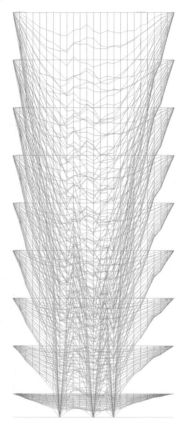

1

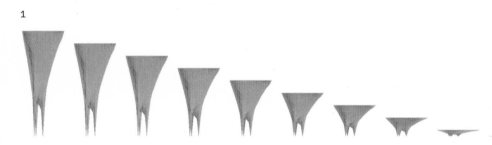

3

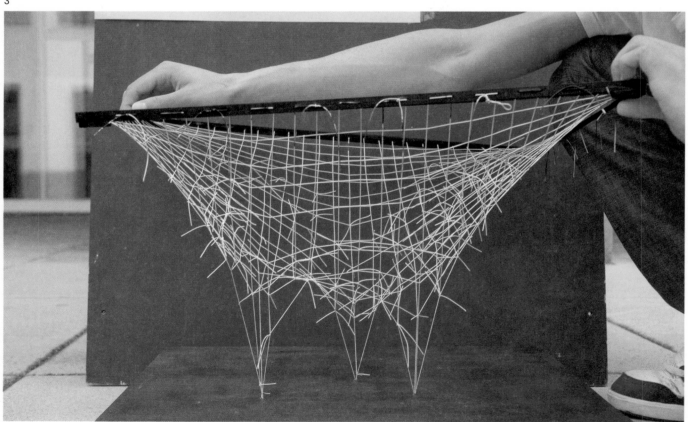

A PHYSICAL CONSTRUCT DECLARING GRAVITY
AT WORK
What appears to be a simple triangulated object
is in fact a structure consisting of bands, with
a hierarchy between the different joints. The
result is not a fully rigid structure but rather a
partially flexible construct that resists gravity
by means of its geometry.

4   Drawing of templates for the construction of the model
5   Cardboard templates
6   Physical model, wood
Nicolas De Courten, Christopher Tan

4

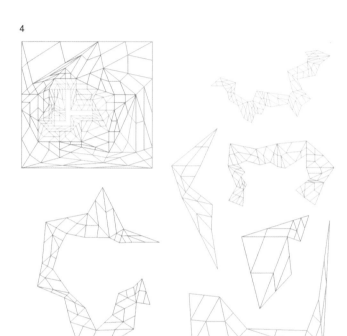

5

6

WORKING MODELS IN TIME
It is a core idea of the ALICE curriculum to work simultaneously in parallel realms—to develop a project in 3-D software and to test it constantly in physical models, or to draw while at the same time probing material qualities in one-to-one mock-ups. In this approach the design process is constantly challenged by catalyst "reactions" in the respective fields of production.

This project was generated through the tracking of a sheet of paper falling in space. The movements were recorded by 3 cameras and then reconstructed in 3-D software. The trajectories of the four cardinal points of the sheet led to a warped spatial construct, built in thin cardboard, its wrapped geometry locking its form in space and making it a structurally robust artifact.
Augusta Prorok, Bertrand Sauterel

1   Sequence drawings: falling paper in space
2   Sequence drawings: volumetric study
3   Physical model declaring gravity at work, paper

1

2

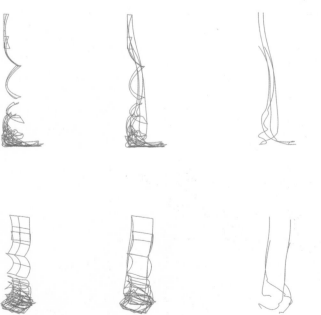

3

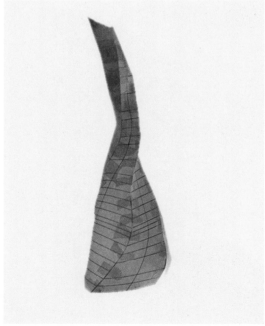

FROM DESIGN DEVELOPMENT TO FABRICATION
The second phase in the ALICE curriculum
tests, transforms, develops and materializes
the initial ideas towards a concrete proposal
for the pavilion. Scale, material, structure,
program, construction details, fabrication and
assembly are addressed.

4,5   Analytical sections in drawing and
model form of a first profane experiment:
a dome of glue, poured over an inflated balloon,
collapsed as the balloon was removed.
Aurel Martin, Mikael Monteserin

6   Gravity impacts on form. A hanging
structure responding to tidal forces along an
embankment. Wood structure connected by
elastic strips.
Fatma Ben Amor, Aurélie Krotoff

4

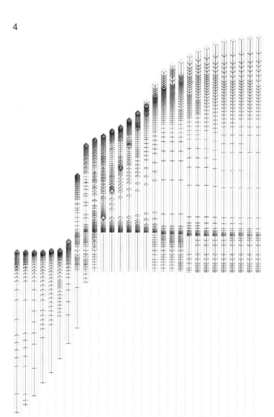

5

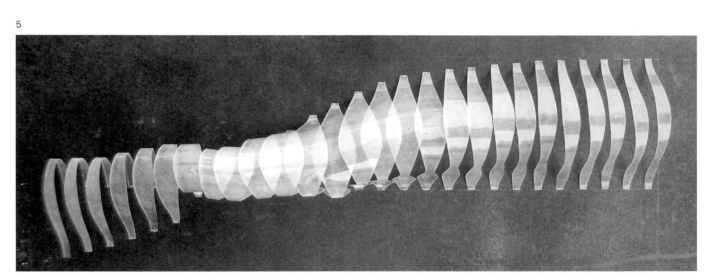

6

This project proposes a physical representation of the spatial impact of a falling object on a series of receivers. In the absence of the falling object, the physical representation registers the temporal aspect of the event while disclosing new spatial encounters.
Adrien Alberti, Sebastien Hefti

1   Physical experiment on gravity: cardboard structure deformed by a stone
2   Rendering of a layered structure derived from physical experiments
3   Physical model, proposal pavilion

1

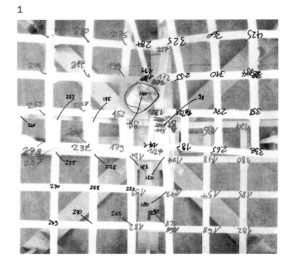

2

3

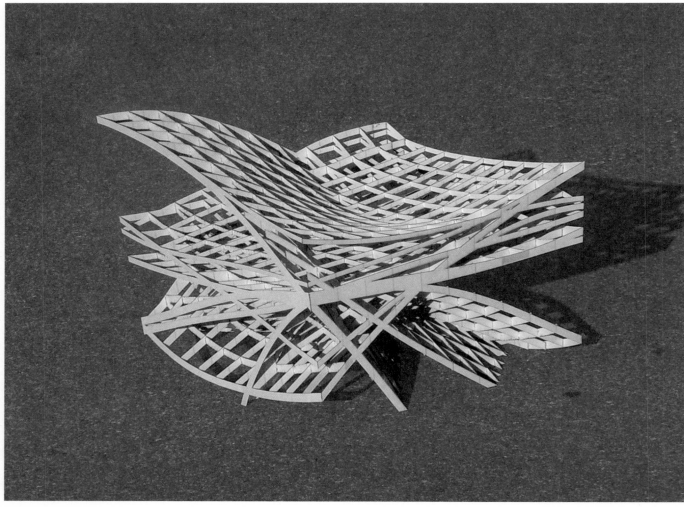

This project was selected by the jury at the end of the first semester. In an extensive discussion with the group, the decision was taken to directly work with the water surface of the River Thames. *Nathalie Egli, Auguste Michael, Andres Tovar Nuez*

4   Physical experiment on gravity: a ball falling into water
5   3-D CAD drawing, section
6   Renderings declaring movement of water

4

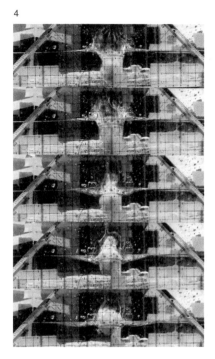

5

6

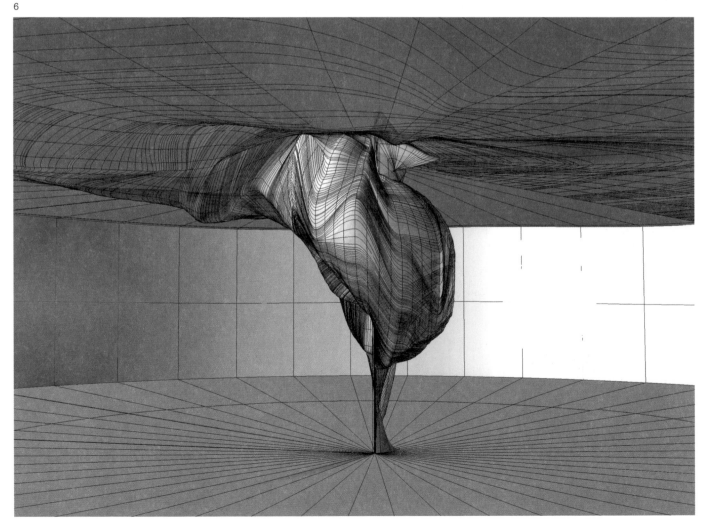

This project and proposal for a pavilion below Millennium Bridge started off with a film sequence of balls impacting on a textile under tension. In the course of the development of the project, the focus shifted from the falling object towards the particular nature of the ground condition.
Clio Gachoud, Minh-Luc Pham

1   Physical experiment on gravity: two falling balls impact on textile under tension
2   Sequence drawings recording the balls in space
3–6   3-D CAD drawing, urban lounge below Millennium Bridge

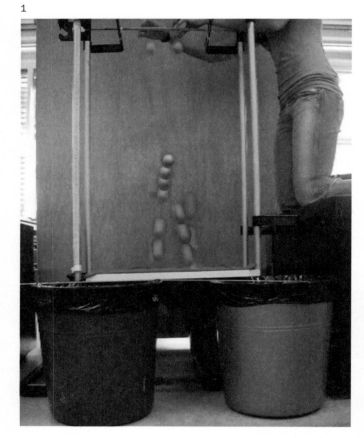

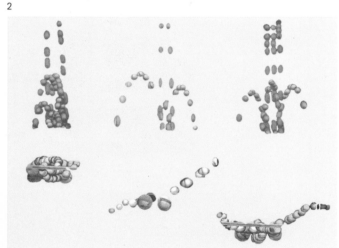

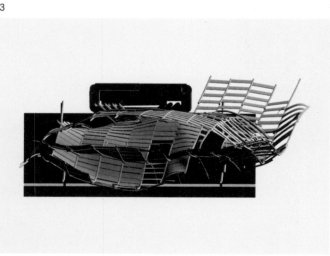

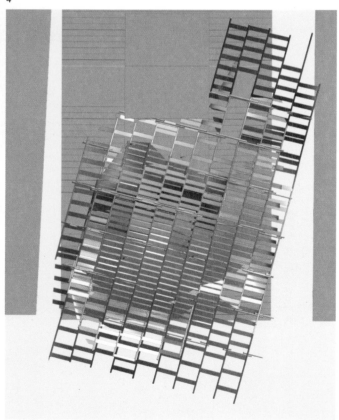

5

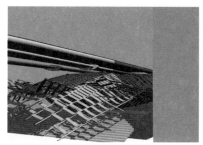

6

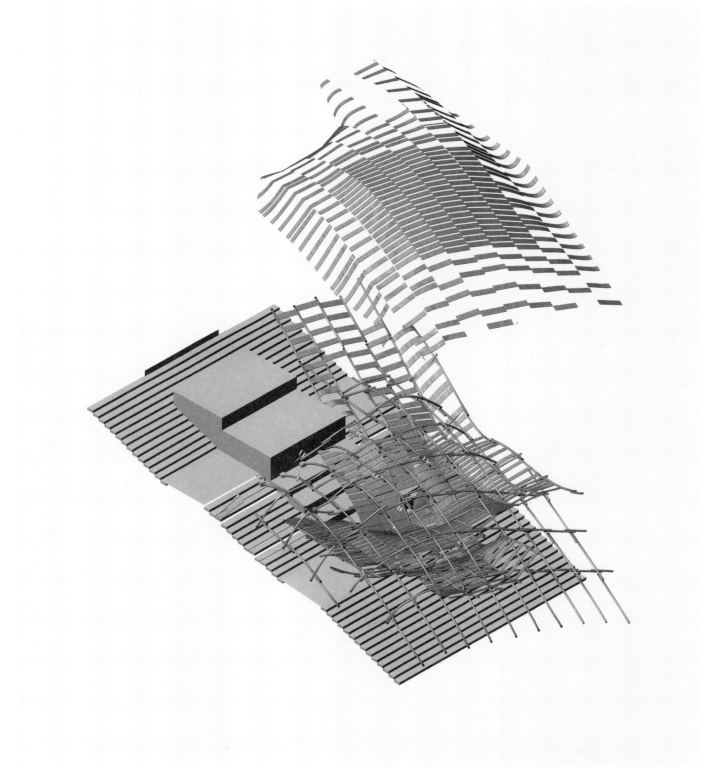

OVERFLOW: THE LONDON PAVILION PROJECT
Overflow was originally designed for Tower Bridge Plaza. This site was strategically chosen in order to investigate how a natural force such as the tidal movement occurring in the Thames could be amplified and extended over the land in the form of a spatial screen, continuously transforming the presence of the iconic London skyline and its perception from the plaza. The pavilion was developed as a group project during the second semester of the ALICE studio.

1–6   The development of the final project was accompanied by a large number of study models, structural tests, mock-ups, and testing materials.

7   Testing a first Styrofoam mock-up: moving with the tide in the river Thames at the embankment of Tower Bridge Plaza in London, March 26, 2008.

1

2

3

4

5

6

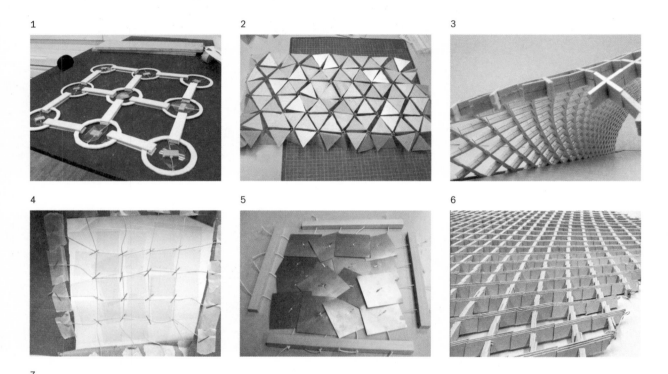

7

The final proposal for the ALICE Pavilion for the London Festival of Architecture is a structure measuring 9 by 15 meters, a large-scale architectonic artifact that interacts with the tidal movements at the Thames River. Conceived as a flexible post-tensioned polystyrene structure fastened along the embankment parapet as a hinge, it will pivot according to the tidal amplitudes in the Thames River.

8   Pavilion project group
9   Rendering of the tidal installation, Tower Bridge Plaza in London

8

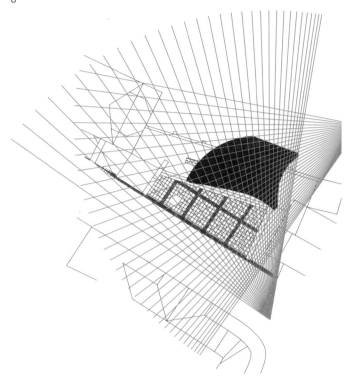

9

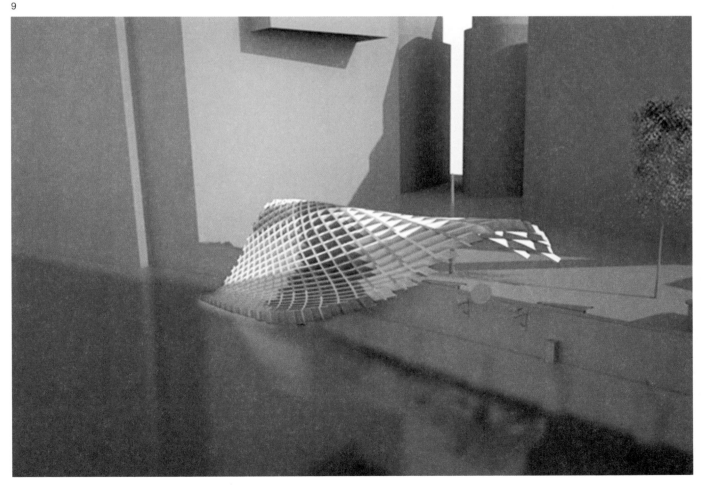

Twelve students took the challenge of bringing the design into fabrication. This took place at the ECAL+EPFL Lab over a period of two weeks and around the clock. Faced with over 800 different pieces to produce, to assemble flat and then to test under various types of forces, the team first had to find strategies for making the cutting process as efficient as possible. This was achieved by means of angle-cut spread sheets that directed a clear path throughout the entire construction process.

1   Production of the structure at ECAL+ EPFL Lab. The demand for space was generously met at ECAL in Renens.
2   *Overflow*, 1:1 test assembly on a football field in Renens near the ECAL+EPFL Lab.

1

2

3   Arrival in London: the stacks with the disassembled members properly placed at the river walkway on June 18, 2008.

4   On June 20, *Overflow* was installed at high tide around 4 P.M. The mounting was staged as a public event. About fifty passersby helped to lift *Overflow* into place and to shift it into its calculated position.

3

4

The structure of the installation is based on the idea of a radial grid. The geometry implies constantly changing viewpoints, as well as porosity in gradient conditions and in motion, caused by the impact of tidal forces. It is specifically designed for passersby in motion. The porosity of the structure will enhance the awareness of the view filtered from behind, implementing a direct awareness of the urban setting.

    1   *Overflow* at low tide, view towards St. Paul's Cathedral

    2a, b   *Overflow* at low tide

    3a, b   *Overflow* at high tide

1

2a

2b

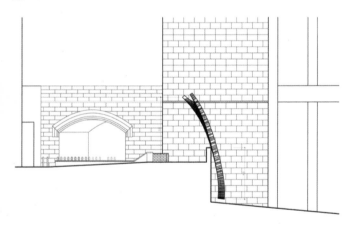

3a

3b

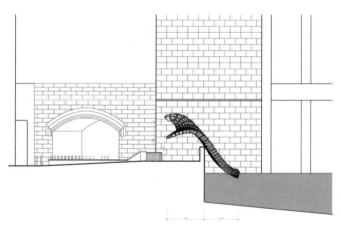

The installation was finally mounted in Southwark at the South Bank of the Thames River in front of Tate Modern. The spatial structure of the installation behaves as a tectonic overflow, from water to land. Although the Thames has historically had a substantial impact on the development of the urban fabric of London, a personal and physical connection to the river is restricted today by an imposing embankment. Twice a day, this buffer zone absorbs an almost unnoticeable water level change of over six meters, mainly vertically along its retaining walls.

4   Frontal view in front of Tate Modern
5a,b *Overflow* at low tide
6a,b *Overflow* at high tide

4

5a

5b

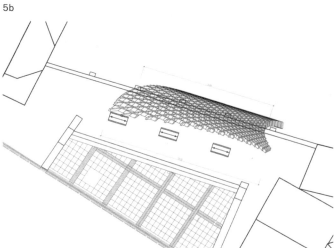

6a

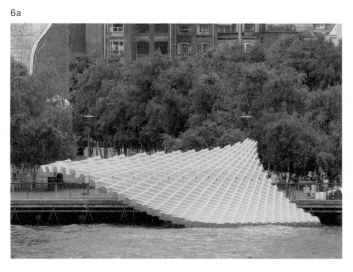

6b

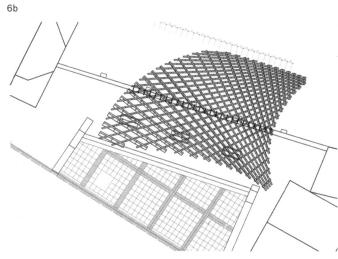

The proposed installation attempts to first ac-
centuate our awareness of the tidal phenomenon
and then transfer it into a physical experience
expanding from a vertical to a horizontal spatial
configuration over the embankment walkway.

1   *Overflow* at low tide
2   *Overflow* at medium tide

1

2

3   *Overflow* at low tide, view towards
St. Paul's Cathedral
   4   *Overflow* at high tide

Pavilion project group: *Malaïca Cimenti, Esteban
Coto Chavarria, Nathalie Egli, Clio Gachoud,
Loïc Jacot-Guillarmod, Auguste Michaud, Monica
Rita Basbouss Moukarzel, Minh-Luc Pham,
Edouard Philippe, Chirstopher Tan, Sandro
Toniett, Andres Tovar-Nuez*

3

4

DIDACTICS   Historical Case Study

STRUCTURE AND CONTENT FOR THE HUMAN
ENVIRONMENT: THE HOCHSCHULE FÜR GESTALTUNG
ULM, 1953–1968

Tilo Richter

From its founding in 1953 until its closure in 1968, The
Hochschule für Gestaltung (HfG) Ulm was considered one
of the most important international centers for the design
of industrial products. Not only did graduates of the HfG
become key players in contemporary product design, but
the pedagogical concept developed at Ulm has had a
lasting influence on the education of designers.

In 1949 Inge Scholl, Otl Aicher and Hans Werner
Richter began to configure an institute at Ulm that was
equally oriented toward politics, science and the humanities. Education in politics and the comprehensive
design of the environment, both in structure and content,
would establish and reinforce humanistic ideals and
democratic thought—nothing less than a "new culture."
During its initial year, the faculty included former Bauhaus
instructors Josef Albers, Johannes Itten, Walter Peter-
hans and Helene Nonné-Schmidt. The first classes were
held in the *Volkshochschule*, while on Oberer Kuhberg
the building for the new institute was being constructed
according to the designs of founding director and former
Bauhaus pupil Max Bill.

When Bill's school buildings were opened in 1955,
Walter Gropius spoke of a "continued, organic development" of the Bauhaus, and the new institute was even
sometimes referred to as "Bauhaus Ulm." However, in
contrast to the legendary Bauhaus of Weimar, Dessau
and Berlin, the teachers and students at Ulm thought
of themselves less as artists and individualists than as
industrial designers, the ones whose task it was to form
and to sustain what Aicher termed the "culture of civi-
lization." Education at the HfG consisted of one year of
basic study and three years of specialization, in product
design, visual communication, construction, information
(until 1964) or film (beginning in 1961). A main objective
common to all subjects was sensitizing students to
cultural and social issues, and scientific and scholarly
approaches accompanied the design process. In the
classrooms, workshops, studios and dormitories designed
by Bill, the cooperative efforts of students and faculty
from around the world reflected the pedagogical approach of the HfG: design, scholarship, and society were
tightly interwoven, and life and work formed a unique
symbiosis.

As its first director, Max Bill primarily influenced
the early years of the HfG. Already by the mid 50s, the
orientation towards the Bauhaus had become the subject
of controversial discussions. The younger instructors
called for a modified curriculum that would make greater

use of science and theory. Tomás Maldonado, an Argen-
tinian who had previously taught in Italy, became an
opponent of Bill, and Bill left the HfG in 1957 as a
reaction to the impending change of course. At the
International Exposition in Brussels in 1958, Maldonado
gave an impassioned speech on the conceptual reorientation of the HfG—the "Ulm model"—which he would
play a decisive role in shaping in the coming years.

From that time on, under a council of directors, the
institute at Ulm became more closely allied with the
production of industrial goods. The new symbiosis of
design and industry was, for example, evident in the
products of Max Braun AG, the renowned manufacturer
of electrical household appliances. Braun's department
of product design, developed by Fritz Eichler, cooperated closely with the HfG, as did Dieter Rams ("Mr. Braun").
Several of the HfG faculty did design work for Braun
directly, such as Hans Gugelot (who designed the SK4,
"Snow White's Coffin," with Dieter Rams), Inge Scholl
and Otl Aicher (Corporate Design). As quickly and in-
tensively as new design ideas flowed into production,
so the experience and knowledge gained there was fed
back into teaching.

According to some of the faculty, in the 1960s the
teaching was becoming increasingly subject to scientific premises. Maldonado and those who had supported
him in the dispute around Aicher and Gugelot now became
the target of opposition. Lecturers such as mathematician
Horst Rittl, sociologist Hanno Kesting and industrial
designer Bruce Archer advocated a strictly analytical
methodology quite distinct from their colleagues' orientation toward industrial practice. In the mid 60s, internal
conflicts around the pedagogical orientation of the HfG
intensified, and were increasingly accompanied by
public criticism. The institute's closure in 1968 was the
result of multiple factors: a lack of political support led
to the elimination of necessary financial subsidies from
the government of Baden-Württemberg, which also had
not been able to offset the considerable debts of the
Scholl Foundation. Gui Bonsiepe, a designer who had
received his diploma from Ulm in 1959, said of the institute in the year of its closing, "Although the HfG did not
meet a heroic end, the hope at its beginning was indeed
heroic. The HfG should not be measured by what it achieved,
but by what it was prevented from achieving."

BIBLIOGRAPHY
• Curdes, Gerhard. *HfG Ulm: 21 Rückblicke. Bauen – Gemein-
schaft – Doktrinen.* Ulm: Verlag Dorothea Rohn-Klewe, 2006.
• Krampen, Martin, and Günther Hörmann. *Die Hochschule für
Gestaltung Ulm – Anfänge eines Projektes der unnachgiebigen
Moderne = The Ulm School of Design – Beginnings of a Project of
Unyielding Modernity.* Berlin: Verlag Ernst & Sohn, 2003.
• Maldonado, Tomás: "Design Education." In *Education of
Vision,* edited by Gyorgy Kepes, 122–135. New York: George
Braziller, 1965.

C HOCHSCHULE FÜR GESTALTUNG ULM *Tilo Richter*

1 Max Bill with Ray and Charles Eames at Ulm, 1955 (Photo: Ernst Hahn)
2 Inge Aicher-Scholl and Walter Gropius at the opening of the HfG campus, 1955 (Photo: Ike and Hannes Rosenberg)

3 Photo studio at HfG, 1957 (Photo: Wolfgang Siol)
4 HfG campus buildings by Max Bill, 1955 (Photo: Wolfgang Siol)

5 Tomás Maldonado teaching, 1966 (Photo: Roland Fürst)
6 Students room in the "Wohnturm" at HfG campus, 1958 (Photo: Wolfgang Siol)

1

2

3

4

5

6

D

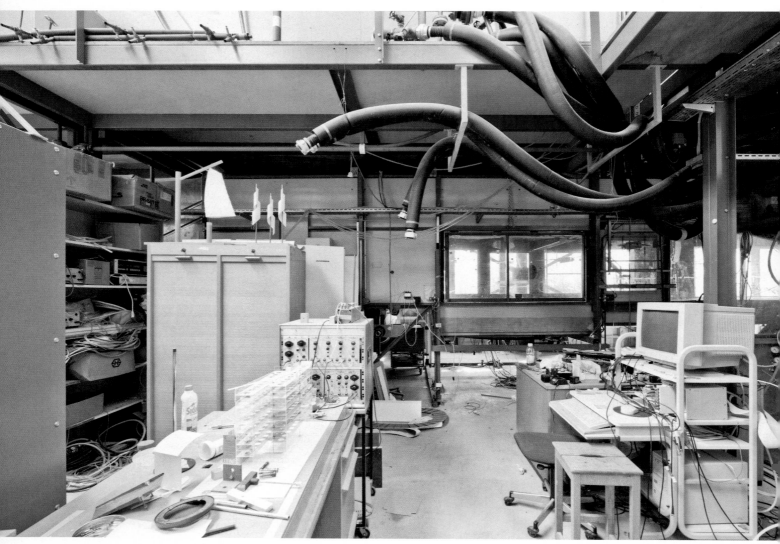

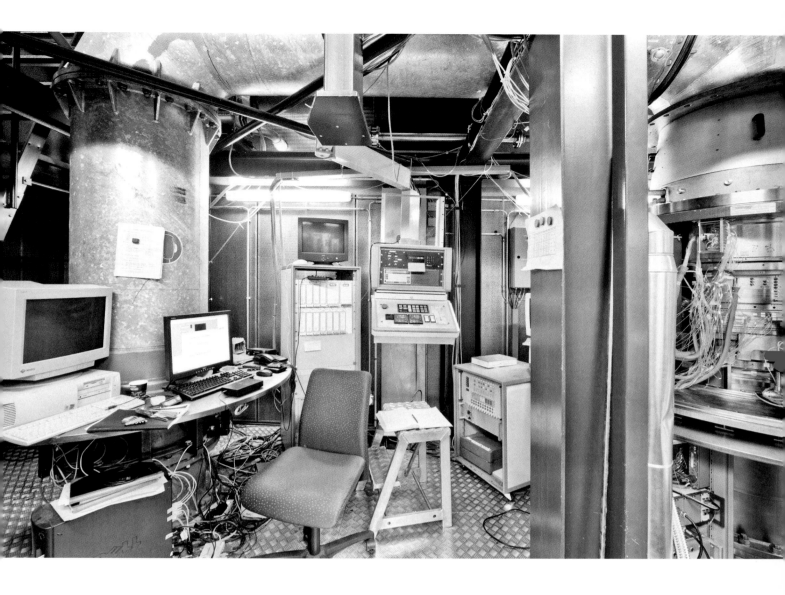

TECHNOLOGY

166

TECHNOLOGY

Essay

ARCHITECTURE AS MEMBRANE

Georges Teyssot

In *The Logic of Sense* (1969), Gilles Deleuze alluded to what Antonin Artaud uttered on leaving the psychiatric hospital in Rodez: "No mouth No tongue No teeth No larynx No oesophagus No stomach No belly No anus I will rebuild the man that I am."[I] This appeal invoked a continuous, fluid body of blood and bone, one not reduced to each of its organs. Later, in *Anti-Oedipus* (1972), Deleuze and Félix Guattari would hypothesize a body conceived as a libidinal machine, a "desiring machine" that points to the theoretical possibility of a "body without organs."

Nowadays, we are confronted by two hypotheses that seem almost mutually exclusive. On the one hand, there is a "body without organs," that is to say a notion of the body not based on the singularity and autonomy of each organ but in which the organs are allegedly indeterminate. On the other hand, there is a notion based on the organic organization of organs, called the "organism," which corresponds to the conventional notion of the body, functioning according to the internal logic and hierarchies that have long dominated physiology and clinical discourse. These two approaches to the explanation of corporeality seem diametrically opposed, yet one does not truly exclude the other. One version favors a "body-without-organ," the (fertile) dream of schizophrenics, which considers the body purely in its *exteriority*, in relation to other bodies, perceived through relationships of surface, difference, affect, and desire, functioning "as a virtual and smooth space, connected with the fluxes and flows that run through and across it."[II] The other version stresses the reality, or normality, of the organism, conceiving the body exclusively in terms of its *interiority*, its regime of internal distribution, in which autonomous organs fragment the whole into multiple parts, breaking up its integrity. This kind of functional logic is reflected, moreover, by what subtends all so-called "modern" architecture, which in fact is nothing other than an application of organicism.

D

In their analysis, Deleuze and Guattari adopted a critical stance with regard to certain trends in psychoanalysis that were influenced by linguistic structuralism. They notably criticized the conception of the body as a *tabula rasa*, a kind of blank slate on which events traced by language could inscribe themselves, and on which power and authority could write the text of the law. This conception of the body—Lacanian, broadly speaking—seemed to involve a punctuation of voided desire by the Signifier, creating a phallic order, namely that of the family, and consequently that of the State. Deleuze and Guattari, in contrast, stressed the fact that desire lacks nothing, that it does not miss its object, that desire and its object are one—one and the same—that desire is a machine and the object of desire is another machine connected to the first one.[III] As they wrote in *A Thousand Plateaus* (1980), Deleuze and Guattari viewed the body as a multifarious surface with skin-like folds: "It is also the skin as envelope or ring, and the sock as reversible surface. It can be a house or part of a house, any number of things, anything. A body without organs is not an empty body stripped of organs, but a body upon which that which serves as organs . . . is distributed according to crowd phenomena, [. . .] in the form of molecular multiplicities."[IV] Within this topology, dwellings come across as something reversible, like the skin of a dead animal or the form of a sock. Forging a new variety of organicism, the interior becomes exterior, while, vice versa, the exterior folds itself into surfaces that may be smooth or striated, folded and unfolding, invaginated or exogastrular.

Nowadays, the "body-without-organs" is confronted with the disturbing prospect of an organ without a body—namely transplants, stored in aptly named organ banks. A disquieting hybrid, the graft is a new species made of flesh and apparatus. Removed from the "donor" organism, a transplant becomes a "free" organ—in other words, available on the open market like any other commodity. Here demand exceeds supply, thus triggering worldwide contraband. A transplant organ is thus *bodiless*—orphaned and celibate, trapped between life and death. It comes from the interval created *between* relational and functional death. Transplant

I   Gilles Deleuze, *The Logic of Sense*, trans. Mark Lester with Charles Stivale (New York: Columbia University Press, 1990).

II   Robert Sasso and Arnaud Villani, eds., "Le Vocabulaire de Gilles Deleuze," *Les Cahiers de Noesis*, vol. 3 (spring 2003): 62.

III   Gilles Deleuze and Félix Guattari, *Anti-Oedipus: Capitalism and Schizophrenia*, trans. Robert Hurley, Mark Seem, and Helen R. Lane (New York: Viking Press, 1977), 26–27.

IV   Gilles Deleuze and Félix Guattari, *A Thousand Plateaus: Capitalism and Schizophrenia*, trans. Brian Massumi (London: Athlone Press), 30.

D

ARCHITECTURE AS MEMBRANE   *Georges Teyssot*

reversible materials, and topological transplants. In fact, just like a Klein bottle—or like an ordinary sock—it is conceivable that this interior will be able to turn itself logically, and topologically, into an exterior. Architecture is thus transformed into a device that participates in this staging of "ecstasy". Given this novel situation, an architectural design no longer leads simply to something to look at (such as an object or building), but rather becomes an apparatus that allows the viewer—i.e. the user—to behold something other than the thing itself.

XIV   Gilles Deleuze, *The Fold: Leibniz and the Baroque*, trans. Tom Conley (Minneapolis: University of Minnesota Press, 1993).

TECHNOLOGY   Historical Case Study

WORLD GAME NEW YORK 1969:
BUCKMINSTER FULLER'S GLOBAL SWITCHBOARD

Mark Wasiuta

"A concrete scientific alternative to politics now exists." Reporting in the *Los Angeles Free Press*, Gene Youngblood delivered his assessment of Buckminster Fuller's World Game seminar. "Played" for the first time during the summer of 1969 at the New York Studio School for Drawing, Painting and Sculpture, the game emerged from Fuller's fixation with managing world resources. For Fuller and the participants the undoubtedly urgent managerial task was only the first move in the more expansive World Game project: to recalibrate global ecological balance, overcome energy scarcity, and fundamentally alter conventional politics. This anti-Malthusian, anti-war game was meant to map a type of perpetual ecological peace and function as an evolutionary acceleration device to usher in a new and total global consciousness.

The game was primarily pedagogical: Fuller postulated that World Game learning was a form of environmental adaptation requisite for planetary survival. Over six weeks, led by Fuller and Edwin Schlossberg, players charted population densities, mineral deposits, "energy slaves," and other data from Fuller and McHale's *World Resource Inventory*, and assimilated them into scenarios for global resource development. Winning strategies graphed results and delineated proposals over sixty-foot-wide Dymaxion maps. The goal was to arrive at the "bare-maximum" conditions under which the global population would have adequate caloric intake to become "globally conscious." Substituting calories for dollars, the game shifted economies of production toward ecological costs and "metaphysical" benefits. Through such structural and perceptual shifts, Fuller envisioned the advent of "design science" and of a new type of subject, "World Man."

The alternative to politics that Youngblood glimpsed in the World Game was perhaps most visible in this new subject constituted by enhanced environmental vision and able to transcend insignificant boundaries and constraints. The New York participants proposed catalyzing caloric growth by linking land masses and underserved populations with information and energy lines across the North Pole, thus offering a solution that both replicated the reach of the military control environment of NORAD and other cold war institutions and yet remained indifferent to those networks' divisions and antagonisms. In Fuller's words, World Man and the World Game were "freed of arbitrary political boundary controls."

Beyond the plane of politics, reoriented World Man and the Sky-Ocean World Projection became homologous. The game prepared a type of ecstatic integration by attempting "to plug in our sensory awareness mechanisms to the switchboard of 'universe' to get in sync with the metabolism of this spaceship's environment." The integration of World Man into the statistical channels and graphs of the gaming surface aimed toward Fuller's ambition of "enveloping" players within a field of data.

The Apollo moon landing was closely monitored by the gamers, who saw a symmetry between World Game's image of earth and photographs of earth shot from space. This symmetry anticipated a radical new perception of the globe—organic, integrated, "fluidic." Yet, this perception simultaneously relied on a technological similarity: NASA's demonstration of complex mission coordination and computation bore a strong resemblance to the World Game fantasy of perfectly administered technologies and resources, a task Fuller, with characteristic numeric certainty, calculated to be 37 times the complexity of Soviet 5-year plans.

The New York game was a "long-hand" prototype for a series of proposed World Game structures from the early Geoscope to the later World Simulation Institute, with its football field sized display, which Fuller argued would provide a spectacle of global information and attract players and viewers via its "photogenic" allure. Even in its modest analog version the Game was "more beautiful than he could have imagined." Fuller no doubt was alluding to the proto-spectacle of the intense play and collective involvement of the gamers. Yet, above all, the beauty referred to a new vision the game would foster. Among Fuller's abiding obsessions was the limited range of the electromagnetic spectrum available to human vision. World Game would serve as a corrective, an optical aid that would render visible environmental data, movement patterns, linguistic relations, or any other structuring condition that normally evaded simple visual perception.

For Fuller, as for other cybernetically inclined environmental designers, a homeostatic natural ecology was paralleled by this newly visible information ecology. In World Game, this latter ecology was oddly positioned in relation to the "closed system" of the planet, both within the whole earth and simulating it, yet continually modifying it in an infinite regress of global data. World Man would not attain integration with the world through projection into harmonious nature, but through recursive information graphing that, in turn, would inscribe him into his natural habitat, World Game.

BIBLIOGRAPHY
• Deren, Mary, and Medard Gabel (eds.). *World Game Report*. New York: The New York Studio School of Painting and Sculpture, 1969.
• Fuller, Richard Buckminster. *The World Game: Integrative Resource Utilization Planning Tool.* Carbondale: World Resources Inventory, Southern Illinois University, 1971.

D   BUCKMINSTER FULLER   *Mark Wasiuta*

1   Edwin Schlossberg addressing
World Game participants at the New York
Studio School, summer 1969.

2   Buckminster Fuller during World
Game participants at the New York Studio
School, summer 1969. Frames from
R. Buckminster Fuller: The World Game,
16 mm film, directed by Herbert Matter,
Saturn Pictures Corp., 1971.

1

2

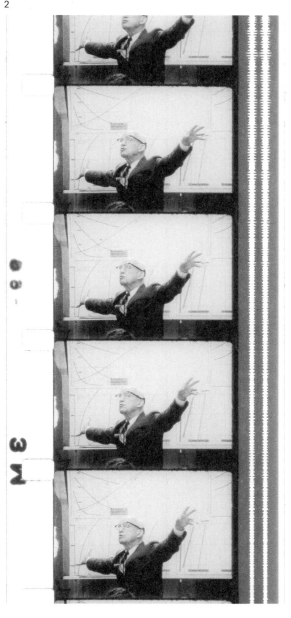

DFAB

Gramazio & Kohler, Architecture and Digital Fabrication
Eidgenössische Technische Hochschule Zürich (ETHZ)

Fabio Gramazio
Matthias Kohler
Tobias Bonwetsch
Ralph Baertschi
Michael Hanak
Nadine Jerchau
Michael Knauß
Daniel Kobel
Michael Lyrenmann
Silvan Oesterle

DIGITAL MATERIALITY IN ARCHITECTURE:
BRIDGING THE REALMS OF THE VIRTUAL AND THE PHYSICAL

Fabio Gramazio and Matthias Kohler

With the term *digital materiality,* we designate an emergent transformation in the expression of architecture. We recognize that materiality is increasingly being enriched with digital characteristics, and these characteristics significantly affect the material nature of built architecture. *Digital materiality* arises through the interaction between digital and material processes during design and construction. The synthesis of these two seemingly distinct worlds—the digital and the material—gives rise to new self-evident realities and sensualities. Data and material, programming, and construction are woven into one another. *Digital fabrication* makes this synthesis possible. It allows the architect of today to weave design data directly into the material building process. In this way, material is enriched with information—it is "informed." In the future, architects will be able to intervene deeply in digital fabrication processes and participate in forming them. This is a new situation: it transforms the possibilities and thus the professional scope of the architect.

SENSUALITY OF DIGITAL ORDER

Digital materiality leads to a new expression and—surprisingly enough, given the technical associations of the term "digital"—to a new sensuality in architecture. It consists in the formation of digital and material orders that mutually overlay and condition one another, and is distinguished by an unusually high number of precisely organized elements, by delicate detailing as well as the parallel presence of different scales of formation. Despite its intrinsic complexity, we experience and understand it intuitively. In doing so, we refer to our experience in reading natural phenomena. *Digital materiality* is not solely anchored in the material world and its principles; to an equal extent, it incorporates the principles of the immaterial world of digital logic, such as its processuality or its mathematical precision. Interestingly, through digital organization, the characteristics of underlying materials are expressed in an intensified form. Materials do not appear primarily as texture or surface, but in their whole depth and plasticity. We discover familiar materials, such as brick—which is more than nine thousand years old—in new manifestations. For the viewer, a tension arises between the intuitively comprehensible properties of a material and a formal logic that is not always evident at first sight. The logic can be felt, but does not impose its own explanation. A variation and multiplicity unfolds that seduces our senses and invites them to linger.

PROGRAMMING CONSTRUCTIONS

Digital materiality arises through the coupling of construction and programming. We take advantage of the conceptual similarities between the fabrication of a building component and the programming of a computer. Computer programs describe the processing of data as a sequence of individual steps in calculation. Likewise, the fabrication of a building component is carried out in a temporal sequence of individual steps. By mapping the *savoir faire* of construction into a programmed process, we can design the fabrication process directly; design and execution are no longer distinct, temporally adjacent phases. The design incorporates the knowledge of its production already at the moment of its conception. In turn, this has the consequence that with digital technology the understanding of construction as an integral part of architectural design takes on greater significance. With digital craftsmanship, we are making a link to the constructive tradition of architecture.

These thoughts lead to the question of whether it makes sense to formalize designs entirely or partially in computer programs, thus notating architectural logics rather than drawing or modeling them. Until this time, as architects we have had little connection to the unfamiliar "language" of programming. The uninitiated perceive it as restrictive because, from the start, it seems to require precise settings. However, to allow this precision to be restrictive on the level of content would be as pointless as capitulating to a freshly sharpened pencil. Because in reality, it is programming itself that provides the necessary instrumental basis to free ourselves from the prevailing images of digital architecture production. The "hands-on" experience of programming allows a demystified understanding of digital technologies and a liberated, autonomous approach to the computer. Through digital craft, we emancipate ourselves from the existing CAAD instruments and the passive implementation of their built-in paradigms— their operations, called up on menus, which are mostly programmed simulations of traditional drawing functions.

VARIATION AND MULTIPLICITY

Digital materiality increases the presence of variation and multiplicity in architecture. These characteristics show themselves at various scales, from materials and building components, to sequences of rooms and support structures, to houses and urban zoning schemes. They arise through the possibility, with digital means, of designing large quantities of elements in a differentiated way. Before the availability of the computer and digital fabrication, these design interventions would not have made any sense, but using today's tools, they can be designed, organized, and built pragmatically. Digital materiality suggests a development trajectory for architecture that will incorporate diverse, complimentary logics weighted relative to each other, rather than being limited to repetition. In the digital age, our conception of serial repetition, which was the product of industrialization, is being transformed much in the same way as the opposing romantic conception of the "natural" uniqueness of craftsmanship. The newly presented aesthetics of differentiated, controlled multiplicity can be readily compared with natural phenomena. It is very appealing to imagine the beginning of a synthetic genesis in analogy to the natural growth of plants or animals; however, there is a temptation to ignore the fact that digital materiality is subject to its own principles unsuitable to biological metaphors. These are the principles of digital logic and program sequencing, which unlike nature proceed without regard to time or environmental influences. The digital is a model world which exists parallel to the physical one. It is the product of a centuries-old culture of dualistic thought. Hence, the multiplicity that attends a design of digital processes seems novel, but not entirely strange, since it refers to familiar experiences of perception. The new forms in all their variety appeal to the senses while continuing to assert their distinctly inorganic derivation.

DYNAMIC RULES INSTEAD OF STATIC PLANS
Digital Materiality leads us beyond the shaping of static forms and images to the design of material processes. There, we relinquish geometry in drawn or modeled form as the central design medium or the actual construction plan of architecture, and also as the basis for its judgment. Instead, we design relationships and sequences that inhere in architecture and become its physical form. As soon as we begin to conceive such material processes, an entirely new way of thinking of architecture is opened up to us. It is a conceptual way of designing with architectural parameters, conditions, relationships, and degrees of freedom. We weigh influences between the form-generating factors. Along the way, the medium of programming allows us to model and control complex sequences of decision-making, and to refine these in an iterative process. The resulting architectural expression is different, because new realities are produced in the medium of design programming. When we design architectures as material processes, we no longer have in front of us a static plan, but instead a dynamic set of rules. We design a behavior. We have the possibility to involve the customer or partner actively in our design, by consciously giving him or her partial control over the final product. We are designing architecture as an open system with different active participants.

Designing with digital technologies interests us because it delineates the boundaries of rationality and predictable reality. In our eyes, architecture is not a profession that can be reduced to optimization, but a multifaceted cultural production. It is *digital materiality* that makes visible the thoroughly human dimension and quality of this production. *Digital materiality* transforms the physis of architecture and may soon also change its image in the eyes of society.

DFAB ROBOT CELL, ETH ZURICH
Research facility with industrial robot. This
offers the possibility—unique in an architectural
context—of processing building elements of
up to 7×3 m at a scale of 1:1, using a variety
of tools specified by the architects themselves.

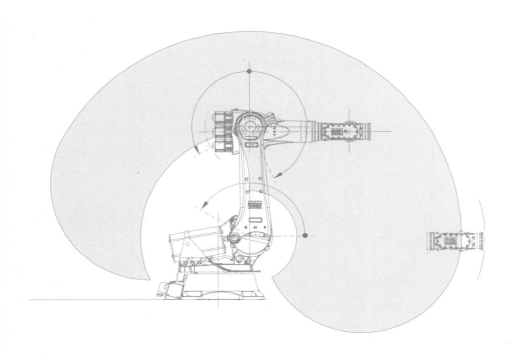

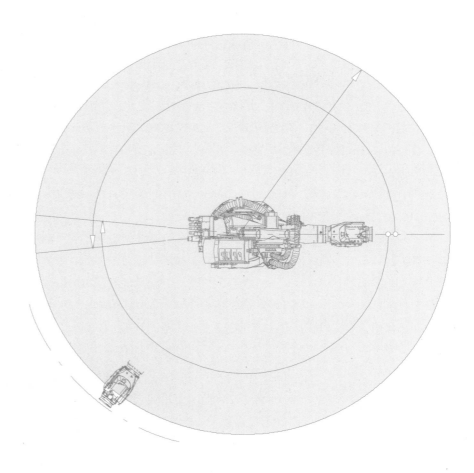

THE PROGRAMMED WALL
Provided that the basic conditions of manufacturing change from manual labor to digital
fabrication, what are the design potentials within
one of architecture's most common elements,
a brick wall? In a workshop we challenged students to design a three-by-two-meter brick wall,
to be produced by an industrial robot. Specific
to the robot is that it can position every brick
differently without additional time or effort.
To make use of this ability the students developed algorithmic design tools that informed
the single bricks of their spatial disposition.
This way they were able to describe a brick wall
in which each of its 400 individual members has
a specified rotation and position in space.
    The results from this workshop contain
both the archaic presence of the material,
as well as the differentiated qualities of their
procedural design. These walls cannot be
designed two-dimensionally or be pictorially
described, but have to be programmed.

The ability to add information to the design
and fabrication process creates a surprisingly
new building component from a familiar and
trusted architectural element.
    1   Physically, the design and fabrication
process is determined by a custom made tool
that is put into the robot's hand and allows him
to perform a specific task, in this case grasping
a brick and placing it precisely in a desired
position.

1

2,3   The programmed designs drew on the knowledge that a masonry bond is a system of rules and regulations that describes the sequence of operations needed to build a wall. The students examined different brick bonds along with criteria for bricklaying, stability, and bonding effect. These findings were transferred into a simple computer script, which they could expand on and refine step by step in an iterative process. The necessary steps and the sequence needed to construct a physical brick wall are reflected directly in the logic of a computer script: a brick is laid on top of another brick, shifted, and perhaps rotated until the end of a row has been reached. This procedure is then shifted half a brick and repeated in the next row until reaching the desired height. When programming, this process is described by two inter-linked loops for the horizontal and the vertical directions. We can easily make use of the computer's ability to perform algorithmic operations in order to induce variations in the positioning of the single bricks.

2

3

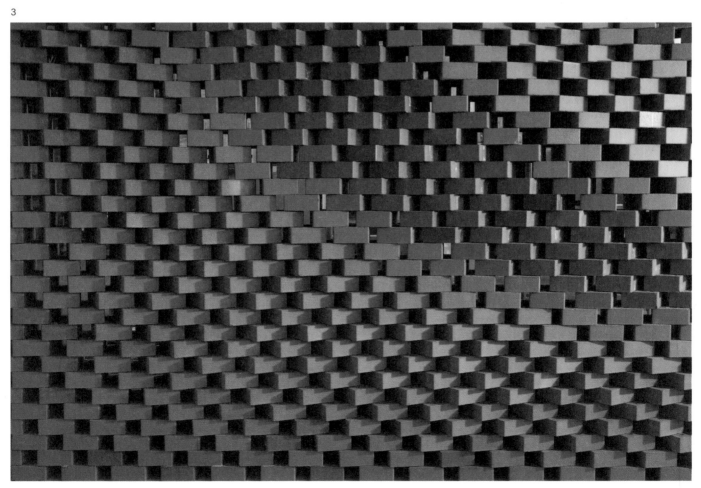

1

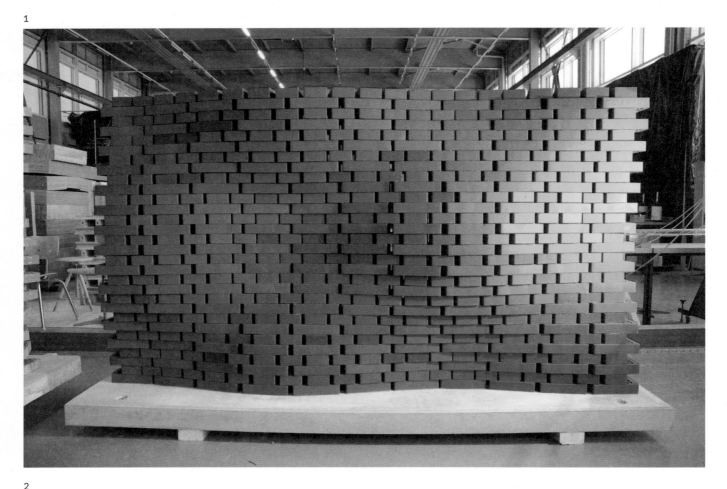

2

1–4   The underlying principle of each realized prototype wall is that the students did not design a geometric system, but rather constructive logics that create an architectural form by organizing material in space and providing the production data directly to the robot. According to this set of data the robot positions every brick as desired.

The prototypes examine architectonic effects, such as the incidence of light and casting of shadows, relief and transparency. They can only be experienced in physical space in relation to time and movement.

ACADEMIC TEAM: *Tobias Bonwetsch, Daniel Kobel, Michael Lyrenmann*
STUDENTS: *Philipp Bollier, Robin Budel, Markus Buehler, Daniel Cajöri, Ursina Götz, Maria Imbach, Michael Knauß, Leonard Kocan, Georg Kummenacher, Daniel Lütolf, Goncales Manteigas, Silvan Oesterle, Daniel Sigg, Florian Stroh, Thomas Summermatter, Matthias Thaler*

3

4

THE RESOLUTION WALL

This project examines the possible use of modules of different sizes for the additive production of building components. Four basic cubic building blocks of aerated concrete in varying dimensions were defined. Starting with a cube-shaped block with an edge of 40 cm, the blocks were halved repeatedly so as to have modules with edges of twenty, ten, and five centimeters. The small modules allow for a dense weave of high-resolution information, whereas the large modules exploit the load bearing capacity of the robot and ensure a fast and economical buildup of mass.

The architectural consequences of the fabrication strategy were first made tangible by the physical prototypes built with the industrial robot. Because a change of resolution is usually accompanied by a change of material, the combination of different sizes of modules at first appears strange and confusing in the homogenous material of one and the same structure. The joint detail conveys a feeling for the procedural logic buried in the depth of the material. One has an idea of the complexity of the construction, yet is no longer able to decipher it.

1

2

1–4 The time needed by the robot to position a module is independent of its size, because the required movement path remains the same. The use of large modules therefore greatly accelerates the building of a wall, but reduces its resolution and thus the possible level of detailing on the surface and in the interior of the component. An intelligent distribution and jointing of different module sizes can resolve the conflict between the aesthetic and functional advantages of the finest resolution, and the economic necessity of the most efficient fabrication process.

3

4

1   A great challenge for the design was to find a suitable packing strategy for the modules of different size, as contradictory requirements of stability, approximation of a desired geometry and an economical construction time had to be met. Therefore, we introduced a genetic algorithm to deal with the large number of possible module combinations. The overall system can be optimized in accordance with an analyzed fitness function. The optimization function results from the need to use the largest possible module, since these require less production time. On the other hand, however, a maximal interlocking between the individual modules has to be achieved, so as to attain an overall stable construction. Thus, numerous iterations of a single design could be generated and evaluated to find and optimized solution. The precise criteria on which the fitness value is based, were part of the investigation.

1

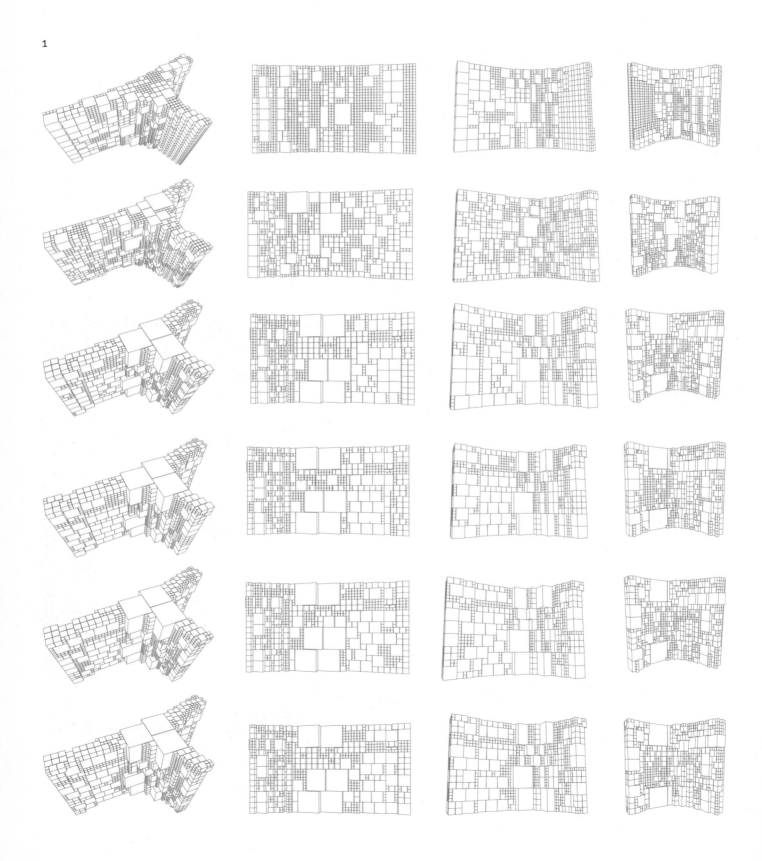

2–4 The different modules merge to form a new whole, whereby fields built of larger blocks enter into a dialog with the areas of finer resolution. At some places these seem as though they are bursting forth from the depth of the element, and at other places as if they are the result of an erosion process.

ACADEMIC TEAM: *Tobias Bonwetsch, Ralph Baertschi, Daniel Kobel, Michael Lyrenmann*
STUDENTS: *Marcia Akerman, Gregor Bieri, Stefan Bischof, Eliza Boganski, Philip Braem, Frank-Olivier Cottier, Irene Lo Iacono, Andreas Kast*

2a

2b

3a

3b

4a

4b

THE FOAM
This project investigated strategies for designing and fabricating panels with polyurethane.
The fascination for researching this additive
material process in combination with digital
fabrication technologies lay in the impossibility
of virtually modeling a process like foaming.
This constraint was seen as an opportunity to
redefine the relation between material potential
and digital tools. The evaluation of design properties only became possible through an iterative
loop of scripting and production. This involved

analyzing the material properties of foam and
its behavior during the foaming process in order
to feed this information back into the design
decisions. The project was organized in small
workshops where students could script and
directly fabricate their designs over several
iterations. In order to control their designs,
parameters such as time, speed, velocity, cen-
trifugal forces and most importantly, the order
in which paths are crossed and overlapped
during the fabrication process, had to be
accounted for.

1

a

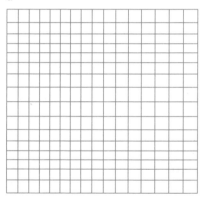

2

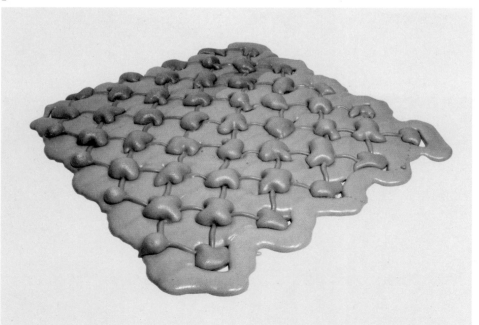

b

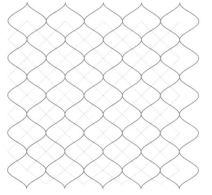

1–4   The material properties of the foam
transform the production information into a
design expression. Depending on speed and line
density, different material effects emerge.
Where pockets accumulate material areas of
growth are defined. If the deposition nozzle
crosses an already cured area, the polyurethane
runs down, creating very fine lines.
  a–d   Digital data showing the paths of
movement that control the robot. Additional
design information such as speed and acceleration are attached to the geometry itself.

3

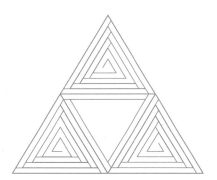

c

4

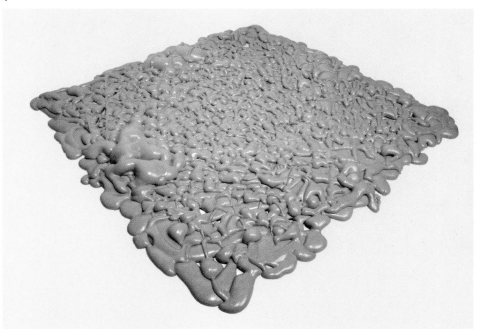

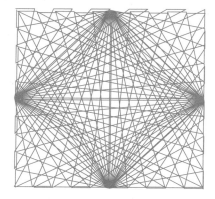

d

1

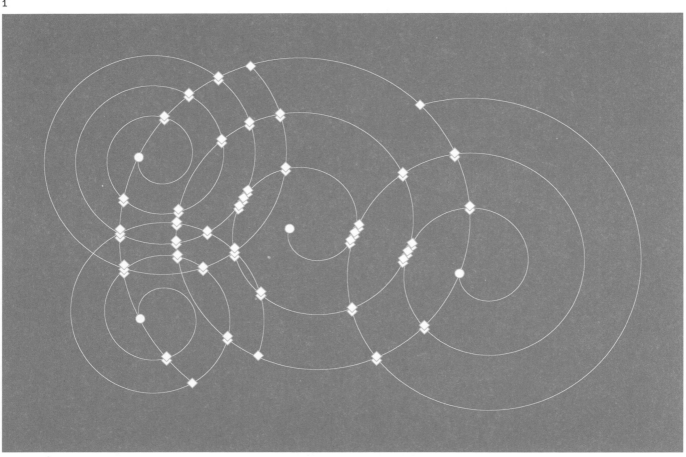

2

1–6   During the second part of the project we examined adopting the foaming process to the design of active acoustic wall panels. The students engaged with the question of how diffuse reflecting acoustic panels will affect the perception of space and the synaesthetic experience between hearing and seeing. Through the application of algorithmic design tools, a parameterized adaption of the acoustic panels to a variety of different spatial as well as acoustical situations became possible.

ACADEMIC TEAM: *Silvan Oesterle, Ralph Bärtschi, Michael Lyrenmann*
EXPERTS: *Juergen Strauss, Acoustic Advisor*
TESTING: *EMPA, Material Science and Technology*
STUDENTS: *Christian Blasimann, Elisa Brusky, Kathrin Hasler, Daniel Hässig, Nils Havelka, Andres Herzog, Kaspar Hofer, Jacob Jansen, Bettina Jochum, Yuta Kanezuka, Simon Kraus, Hannes Oswald, Christoph Rauhut, Michael Reiterer, Sibèlle Urben, Aline Vuilliomenet, Philipp Zimmer, Barbara Zwicky*

3

4

5

6

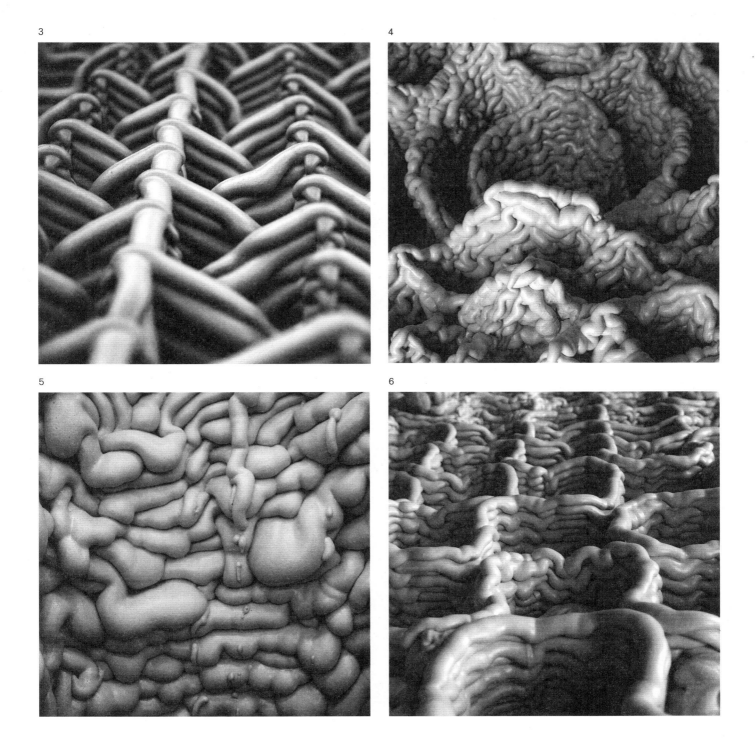

THE SEQUENTIAL WALL
1–5   This project uses wood slats as its basic building element. In contrast to previous projects, the module becomes flexible in one dimension through defining the desired length of each slat. After cutting the length, the robot places the slat at its final position in space. In addition to this flexibility, parameters like load bearing capacity and insulation values as well as the wood-specific parameter of weather protection had to be addressed. The goal was to see performance criteria as a driver and integral part of the configuration: functional aspects of the walls and their aesthetic appearance are directly related and influence each other. This was achieved through abstracting practical requirements and design intentions into design systems, which, in a second step, were translated into computer algorithms. An example for this approach is weather protection. This global parameter dependent on orientation and tilt of a wall element is linked to the length and orientation of the slats, which shield the structural parts of the wall from rain and wind.

1

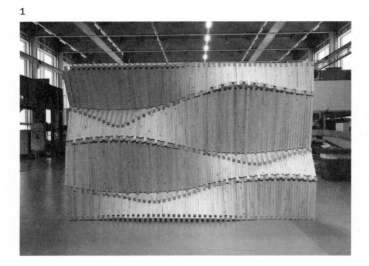

2

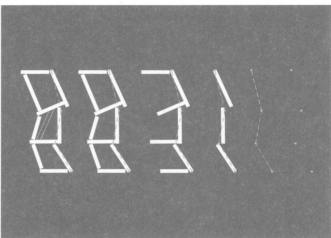

3

4

5

1–3 This design rethinks the traditional notion of porosity and closure within a building envelope. The question was how to combine these different requirements within a unified design framework. The students set out to construct a design tool which would allow them to use input surfaces within a standard 3-D modeling application as the basis for their design. In areas where these surfaces overlap, the placement logic of the slats jumps from being closed to being porous. This approach required precise control of the intersection point, where the open system switches into the closed system and vice versa. It was achieved through a spring system which negotiated the relation of the slat length to its direct neighbors in the layer above, below and at the intersection point.

4–6 Structure, weather protection and insulation are combined to form an integrated whole. The orientation of the slat and its arrangement are based on the materials' requirement not to expose the slat's front end to water. The overhangs between the undulating surface patches prevent water from entering the interior insulation space of the wall. The rippling of the slat structure provides for channeling the water while it flows off the wall and at the same time allows for a connection to the inner structural framework. The visual effect of the wall, carried through the insulation layer to the interior side of the wall, is generated through these functional requirements.

1

2

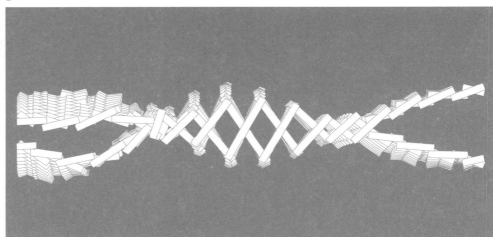

3

ACADEMIC TEAM: *Silvan Oesterle,
Ralph Bärtschi, Michael Lyrenmann*
STUDENTS: *Michael Bühler, David Dalsass,
Simon Filler, Milena Isler, Roman Kallweit,
Morten Krog, Ellen Leuenberger, Jonas
Nauwelaertz de Agé, Jonathan Roider, Steffen
Samberger, André Schmid, Chantal Thomet,
Rafael Venetz, Nik Werenfels*

4

5

6

TECHNOLOGY   Historical Case Study

R AND D: THE EAMES OFFICE AT WORK

John Harwood

Charles and Ray Eames's well known 1943 design for a leg splint for the US Navy is often cited as a masterpiece of rational design—an elegant solution to a problem using minimal means—and as a precursor to their office's later, legendary bent plywood furniture designs. Less frequently mentioned is the fact that the design and production of the splint marks the first time that the Eames Office participated fully in a collaboration between the state and private enterprise. Indeed, the Eameses were inventors in their own right: the famous Kazam! Machine, built in their own apartment in 1941, allowed them to create the signature compound curve plywood surface/structure element. Yet the splint was also an early instance of the new configuration of the human sciences that would become known as *ergonomics*: involving the collaborative efforts of a doctor, manufacturers and military officers, this process of research and development (R&D) allowed the Eameses to expand their design practice from the construction of experimental one-offs to an industrially efficient and medically sanctioned mass product. In this synthetic discipline, the first of many to emerge from the superheated interdisciplinary exchanges that characterized the war effort, the designer was to serve as an equal partner with scientists and engineers in researching and developing products that would help to save "man" from an ever more "hostile environment."

After the war, the research function of the Eames Office continued to expand, with a growing number of commissions from high-technology corporations and government offices. By the mid-1950s, the Eames Office library contained hundreds of volumes on scientific research. According to Parke Meeke, one of the leading designers and technicians in the office, there were many more such volumes than there were books on architecture or industrial design. (The latter were of little use, since they simply documented solutions to "other problems.") The Eames Office archive at the Library of Congress is filled with the artifacts of a lifetime of sustained interdisciplinary research conducted in tandem with the central scientific institutions of the post-WWII period, public and private. RAND Corporation scientists, ARPA researchers, and IBM engineers were often at work elbow-to-elbow with designers in the Eames Office. The contemporary architectural researcher—whether designer, historian or theorist—must therefore grapple with Charles Eames's puzzling axiom that "Everything is Architecture" through a similar investigation of the apparently extra-architectural apparatus of military-industrial research.

That the Eames Office kept itself up-to-date on the cutting-edge scientific research of the day is important, not least for the what it adds to our impression of the depth, rigor and complexity of the office's designs; but it is also essential to note that the research function of the Eames Office did not merely serve to provide raw material or data with which to design. Corporations and government agencies hired the Eames Office to make their research legible to an often skeptical public through the whimsical yet rich exhibitions and product designs for which the office is now justifiably famous, and these same corporations invited the Eames Office to participate actively in their R&D programs. The Eames Office devoted ten years to an unfinished project to design an "IBM Information Center" (also known as the "IBM Museum") intended as a fully computerized laboratory for behavioral experiments on visitors learning about and through technology. The office and IBM scientists imagined it as a *heuristic* environment, "placing a pupil, as far as possible, in the position of a discoverer." In short, in the Eames Office, research itself was increasingly the subject of research.

The project was eventually cancelled due to funding concerns, but the massive amount of research and design that the Eames Office had produced was channeled into an exhibition at IBM's New York headquarters in 1971. The show, entitled *A Computer Perspective*, presented a densely packed history of computing technology (the "History Wall," designed in collaboration with Harvard historian of science I. Bernard Cohen) and experimental exhibits introducing visitors to computing technology through multi-media sensory overload (e.g. the "Communications Rack").

Whatever one's attitude towards the Eames Office's engagement with the research apparatus of the military-industrial complex, its sustained endeavor to come to terms with the implications for design of radically new modes of scientific and technological research is of the utmost importance for understanding both the techniques and the stakes of architectural research today.

BIBLIOGRAPHY
• Latour, Bruno, and Steve Woolgar. *Laboratory Life: The Construction of Scientific Facts*. Beverly Hills: Sage Publications, 1979; reprint Princeton: Princeton University Press, 1986.
• Neuhart, John, Marilyn Neuhart, and Ray Eames: *Eames Design: The Work of the Office of Charles and Ray Eames*. New York: Harry N. Abrams, 1989.
• Office of Charles and Ray Eames: *A Computer Perspective*. Cambridge MA: Harvard University Press, 1973.
• Pugh, Emerson. *Building IBM: Shaping and Industry and its Technology*. Cambridge MA: MIT Press, 1995.

D EAMES OFFICE *John Harwood*

1   Eames Office, panels from the "History Wall" at the exhibition *A Computer Perspective* at IBM Building, New York, 1971.
2   Eames Office, Leg Splint, 1943.

3, 4   Eames Office, designs for floor tile for "Communications Rack" at the exhibition *A Computer Perspective* at IBM Building, New York, 1971.

5   Eames Office and Kevin Roche, IBM Museum project, 1968. View of model.

2
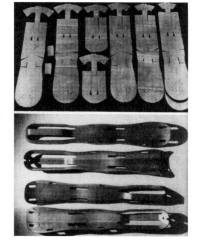

1

3
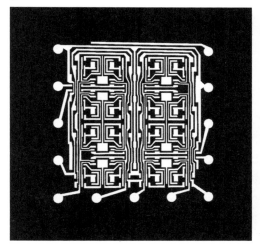

4
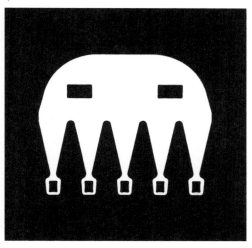

5

LAPA
Laboratoire de la production d'architecture
Ecole Polytechnique Fédérale de Lausanne (EPFL)

FACULTY
Harry Gugger, Ralph Blättler, Simon Chessex,
Jorge Pena Diaz, Enrique Fernandez,
Simon Frommenwiler, Russell Loveridge,
Henriette Spoerl

ADVISORY BOARD
Mario Coyula, Adriana Rabinovich,
Christian Schmid

EXHIBITED PROJECTS
Florian Chazeau, Nathanaël Chollet,
Maxime Duvoisin, Carmen Ebneter,
Yann Gramegna, Mio Tsuneyama

CUBAN STUDENT TEAM 10DE10
Carmen Pons Piedra, Aylin Pascual González,
Yamil Roldán Herrera, Emil Cruz Ortega,
Misleidys Morales Funes, Florencia Medina,
Sergio Valdés, Sandra Becerra Carbó,
Oliesky Fabre del Castillo, Lázaro Fernández
Vázquez, Ennis Carralero Fernández,
Yaratzel Gutiérrez Martínez, Yosbel Hernández
Peñate, Daniel Moliner, María José Fernandez,
Iruma Rodriguez

SWISS STUDENT TEAM 10DE10
Tiago Mendes, Isabel Oliveira, Jérémy Trieu,
Marnie Amato, Frédéric Karam, Alexandre
Vergères, Nadine Schmied, Mélanie Monks,
Hendrik van Boetzelaer, Julien Ecoffrey,
Joana Varela, Wing-Chung Cheung,
Léonard Gurtner, Miguel Marques,
Nicole Giambonini, Lucas Cohen-Adad,
Deborah Eker

MAS UD
Master of Advanced Studies in Urban Design
Eidgenössische Technische Hochschule Zürich (ETHZ)

FACULTY (SNF SCHWYZ AND MAS URBAN DESIGN)
Marc Angélil, Philippe Cabane, Sascha Delz,
Kathrin Gimmel, Dirk Hebel, Darius Karácsony,
Noboru Kawagishi, Tobias Klauser, Lukas Küng,
Patrick Maisano, Michael Martin, Martin Matter,
Deane Simpson, Jörg Stollmann, Dawit Benti,
Zegeye Cherenet, Bisrat Kifle

STUDENTS – 2006/2007
Sebastiàn Alfaro Fuscaldo, Iva Cuzela-Bilac,
Fei Duan, Noboru Kawagishi, Daphne Kokkinni,
Christine Mayr-Baldauf, Theano Mazaraki,
Imke Annemarie Mumm, Ha Thi-Thanh Nguyen,
Dimitra Riza, Stefanie Scherrer,
Matthew Gerald Skjonsberg, Krishnan Varma

STUDENTS – 2007/2008
Theodora Christina Balauru, Charis Christodoulou,
Tibebu Daniel Desta, Zografia Karekou,
Simon Kramer Vrscaj, Christiane Lange,
Sander Laureys, Anne Charlotte Matherre-Barthes,
Konrad Milton, Raul Alberto Marino Zamudio,
José Ortega Rodriguez, Hyeri Park,
Brook Teklehaimanot Haileselassie, Lina Zhang,
Angeliki Zisimopoulou

ALICE
Atelier de la conception de l'espace
Ecole Polytechnique Fédérale de Lausanne (EPFL)

FACULTY
*Dieter Dietz, Aline Dubach, Eveline Galatis,
Olivier Ottevaere, Isabella Pasqualini,
Daniel Pokora, Katia Ritz, Marc Schmit*

STUDENTS—OVERFLOW
*Malaïca Cimenti, Esteban Coto Chavarria,
Nathalie Egli, Clio Gachoud, Loïc Jacot-Guillarmod,
Auguste Michaud, Monica Rita Basbouss Moukarzel,
Minh-Luc Pham, Edouard Philippe, Chirstopher Tan,
Sandro Toniett, Andres Tovar-Nuez*

STUDENTS—THE LIGHTHOUSE PROJECT
*Adrien Alberti, Martin Aurel, Dorette Baumann,
Matthias Bellmann, Fatma Ben Amor,
Nicolas de Courten, Konstantinos Dell'Olivo,
An-Madlen Gfeller, Andreas Gubler, Axel Harari,
Steffan Heath, Sebastian Hefti, Lila Held,
Alexander Hertel, Thaddée Lucan, Aurélie Krotoff,
Patrick Meier, Mikael Monteserin, Jakob Phillipp,
Augusta Prorok, Bertrand Sauterel*

DFAB
Gramazio & Kohler, Architecture and Digital Fabrication
Eidgenössische Technische Hochschule Zürich (ETHZ)

FACULTY
*Fabio Gramazio, Matthias Kohler, Tobias Bonwetsch,
Ralph Baertschi, Michael Hanak, Nadine Jerchau,
Michael Knauß, Daniel Kobel, Michael Lyrenmann,
Silvan Oesterle*

STUDENTS
*Marcia Akermann, Gregor Bieri, Stefan Bischof,
Christian Blasimann, Eliza Boganski, Elisa Brusky,
Matthias Buehler, Michael Bühler, Philip Braem,
Clarence Chia Tien San, Frank-Olivier Cottier,
David Dalsass, Ramirez Daniel, Simon Filler,
Kathrin Hasler, Daniel Hässig, Nils Havelka,
Andres Herzog, Kaspar Hofer, Irene Lo Iacono,
Milena Isler, Jacob Jansen, Bettina Jochum,
Christoph Junk, Roman Kallweit, Yuta Kanezuka,
Andreas Kast, Michael Knauss, Leon Kocan,
Simon Kraus, Morten Krog, Ellen Leuenberger,
Daniel Lütolf, Jonas Nauwelaertz de Agé,
Silvan Oesterle, Hannes Oswald,
Goncales Manteigas, Christoph Rauhut,
Michael Reiterer, Jonathan Roider,
Steffen Samberger, Andre Schmid, Dominik Sigg,
Chantal Thomet, Sibèlle Urben, Rafael Venetz,
Aline Vuilliomenet, Pascal Waldburger,
Nik Werenfels, Libei Zhao, Philipp Zimmer,
Barbara Zwicky*

- *Marc Angélil* is a professor at the Department of Architecture at ETH Zurich. He is the author of several books, including *Inchoate: An Experiment in Architectural Education* and *Indizien: Zur politischen Ökonomie urbaner Territorien* (on the political economy of contemporary urban territories).

- *Tom Avermaete*, an associate professor at the Delft University of Technology, is the author of *Another Modern: The Post-War Architecture and Urbanism of Candilis-Josic-Woods*. He is an editor of *OASE Architectural Journal* and works on the research project "In the Desert of Modernity: Colonial Planning and After."

- *Daniel Bisig* holds a research position at the Artificial Intelligence Laboratory of the University of Zurich and at the Institute for Computer Music and Sound Technology of the Zurich University of the Arts. He realizes projects at the intersection of new media and artificial life.

- *Dieter Dietz* is an architect, founding member and partner at UNDEND Architecture in Zurich. He is currently an associate professor of Architectural Design at EPFL/ENAC School of Architecture, Civil and Environmental Engineering in Lausanne.

- *Angelus Eisinger*, an urban historian and urbanist, holds the chair for History and Culture of the Metropolis at Hafen City University in Hamburg. With his practice, Perimeter Stadt, he is also involved in consulting and conceptual work in urban planning competitions and studies.

- *Ole W. Fischer* teaches theory of architecture at ETH Zurich. In his PhD thesis he analyzed Henry van de Velde's artistic and theoretical work dedicated to Friedrich Nietzsche. He is a co-editor of the book *Precisions: Architecture between Sciences and the Arts*.

- *Kim Förster* is a PhD candidate and an assistant in architectural theory at the ETH Zurich, where he is writing a thesis on the Institute for Architecture and Urban Studies, New York (1967–1984). Since 2002, he has co-edited the architectural journal *An Architektur*.

- *Filip Geerts* is an architect and an assistant professor at the Delft University of Technology, where he is presently working on his PhD ("Architecture/Territory").

- *Reto Geiser*, an architect trained at ETH Zurich, is completing his doctoral dissertation on issues of cultural transfer in the work of Sigfried Giedion. He is the curator of the Swiss Pavilion at the 11th Venice Architecture Biennale.

- *Andri Gerber*, currently an assistant professor at the Ecole Spéciale d'Architecture in Paris, holds a PhD from ETH Zurich ("Urban Metaphors").

- *Fabio Gramazio* is partner at Gramazio & Kohler Architects and assistant professor for Architecture and Digital Fabrication at the ETH Zurich. Gramazio & Kohler are the authors of the book *Digital Materiality in Architecture*.

- *Harry Gugger* is partner at Herzog & de Meuron Architects. He created the Laboratoire de la production d'architecture at EPFL/ENAC School of Architecture, Civil and Environmental Engineering in Lausanne.

- *John Harwood* is an assistant professor of Modern and Contemporary Architectural History at Oberlin College. He is currently at work on a book manuscript, "The Redesign of Design: Computer, Architect, Corporation."

- *Philipp Herrmann*, born in Munich, studied graphic design at Zurich University of the Arts. He works as an independent graphic designer in Zurich.

- *Martin Josephy* is an architect, urbanist, and critic based in Basel. He is an executive member of the Virtual Upperrhine University of Architecture (VUUA), a regional network involving architecture and other spatial practices.

- *Jeannie Kim* is the manager of the National Design Awards at Cooper-Hewitt, New York. She has taught at the Harvard University Graduate School of Design and Columbia University Graduate School of Architecture, where she was also the director of Print Publications.

- *Matthias Kohler* is partner at Gramazio & Kohler Architects and assistant professor for Architecture and Digital Fabrication at the ETH Zurich. Gramazio & Kohler are the authors of the book *Digital Materiality in Architecture*.

- *Sanford Kwinter*, a **New** York based writer and theorist, holds a PhD in comparative literature from Columbia University. He is associate professor at Rice University and is currently teaching at Harvard University's GSD. He has written widely on philosophical issues of design, architecture and urbanism.

- *Bruno Latour* was trained as a philosopher and an anthropologist. A former professor at the Centre Sociologie de l'Innovation at the Ecole Nationale Supérieure des Mines in Paris, he is now a professor and vice president for research at Sciences Po Paris.
- *Maris Mezulis* collaborates with architects, designers and technical specialists to create dynamic compositions for and about space. His documentary photos and videos regularly circulate in publications and exhibitions.
- *Rolf Pfeifer* has been the director of the Artificial Intelligence Laboratory at the University of Zurich since 1987. He is a pioneer of the concept of embodiment and the author of *How the Body Shapes the Way We Think*.
- *Tilo Richter*, an architectural and art historian based in Basel, has worked as an author, editor, and book designer since 1995. He holds a PhD from ETH Zurich and is an art market correspondent for the *Frankfurter Allgemeine Zeitung*.
- *Deane Simpson*, an architect, has taught at the ETH Zürich since 2004. He was an associate with Diller + Scofidio in New York between 1997 and 2003. He has published several essays and is a co-author of *The Ciliary Function*.
- *Cary Siress* is a faculty member in Architecture at the School of Arts, Culture, and Environment of The University of Edinburgh and a visiting professor at the University of Nanjing, China. He previously taught at the ETH Zurich, where he completed his PhD.
- *Carolin Stapenhorst* studied architecture at the RWTH in Aachen, Germany. She works as an architect in Italy and is currently a PhD candidate at the Technical University of Turin. She frequented the LAPA studio in 2007/2008, studying its specific design method.
- *Urs Staub* is trained as an art historian, archeologist, and theologian. He is head of the Art and Design division at the Swiss Federal Office of Culture. In this capacity, he is responsible for the advancement of art and design, and is also in charge of the Swiss national art collections and art museums.
- *Martino Stierli* is a postdoctoral fellow at the NCCR Iconic Criticism (eikones) at the University of Basel. He studied art history and holds a PhD from ETH Zurich. He currently teaches at the University of Zurich and is preparing the international exhibition "Las Vegas Studio: Images from the Archives of Venturi and Scott Brown."
- *Georges Teyssot* has taught at Princeton University, where he directed the PhD program in architecture, and presently teaches at Laval University, Quebec. He was curator of the exhibition "The American Lawn" at the Canadian Center for Architecture (CCA).
- *Ludovic Innocent Varone* is a Swiss graphic designer trained at Zurich University of the Arts. He has been working at NORM since 2006 and for Velotto since 2003.
- *Mark Wasiuta* is an associate adjunct professor at Columbia University, Graduate School of Architecture, Planning and Preservation, where he is also director of Exhibitions. He is currently a doctoral candidate at Harvard University and partner at the office International House of Architecture.
- *Albena Yaneva* holds a doctoral degree in sociology from Ecole des Mines de Paris. She is a lecturer in Architectural Studies at the Manchester Architecture Research Center. Her research and teaching involves a socio-technical approach to architecture.

This publication and the exhibition at the Swiss Pavilion at the 11ᵗʰ International Architecture Exhibition in Venice would have not been possible without the generous support of the following patrons and sponsors:

ETH Board, Board of the Swiss Federal Institutes of Technology
EPF Lausanne, ENAC, School of Architecture,
Civil and Environmental Engineering
ETH Zurich, Faculty of Architecture
ETH Zurich, Network City and Landscape (NSL)

Acomet SA
Alcan Composites
BBZ AG
Fondation Braillard Architectes
Gesellschaft für Technische Zusammenarbeit (GTZ)
Holcim Foundation for Sustainable Construction
IBZ Industrie AG
Keller AG Ziegeleien
KUKA
Maagtechnic
Scobalit AG
Sika Schweiz AG
Swisspor SA

Historical Case Study

EXPERIMENTAL WORKSHOP OF MODERNITY:
REFORMIST DESIGN EDUCATION FROM VAN DE VELDE
TO BAUHAUS

Ole W. Fischer

When in 1915 the Grand Ducal School of Applied Arts (Grossherzoglich-Sächsische Kunstgewerbeschule) closed down because of World War I, its former director Henry van de Velde (1863–1957) was asked by the royal authorities to name possible successors. Among others, he suggested the young *Werkbund* architect Walter Gropius (1883–1969). Although relations were venomous between the Grand Duke and van de Velde, and the latter, a Belgian, was regarded as an "enemy citizen", the court followed his advice and commissioned Gropius to propose a concept for reopening the school after the war. In the aftermath of revolution and with the help of the new provisionary government, this led to the founding of the famous "Bauhaus" in March 1919—in the built as well as pedagogical structures established by van de Velde.

At the turn of the twentieth century, a new cultural Weimar movement was gaining momentum with the intention, using Nietzschean philosophy, to reform style following the classical literary epoch of Goethe and Schiller and the musical "silver age" of Franz Liszt. Under the influence of the idea of this movement, the young Grand Duke had appointed the Flemish artist, artisan and architect Henry van Velde as "advisor for the enhancement of the arts." From the beginning of his tenure at Weimar in 1902, van de Velde cooperated with local workshops and manufacturers in the "Seminar of Applied Arts," a free advisory center for design open to craftsmen and industrial model draftsmen of the grand duchy. Unsatisfied with the limited impact on artistic production at large, van de Velde proposed permanent apprenticeships and experimental workshops according to a reform model of artistic education freed from the historic eclecticism that was predominant at art academies, universities and polytechnics. The result, the School of Applied Arts, was successfully established in 1908. As founding director he oriented these workshops around "living projects," not only to provide the school with additional funding, since it struggled with limited resources from the start, but also to approximate for the students an ideal unity of theory, drawing and first-hand experience with material production. To this end, he equipped the school, endowed by his patrons, with modern production facilities, machines and materials and introduced craftsmen as "masters" of the various techniques. Well aware of the restrictions of the curriculum and dangerous fixation on his person, van de Velde fought to merge his school of applied arts with the older Academy of Fine Arts in order to create a new type of design education that would overcome the traditional separation of artists and artisans as well as the disciplinary boundaries of arts, crafts and industry. However, would have to leave the realization of unified design education to Gropius and the Bauhaus, where the preliminary course, the apprentice workshops, the "master" craftsmen and even the machinery were taken over and became part of a modernist pedagogic module style in place at HfG Ulm or IIT Chicago.

Van de Velde theorized this reformist ideal long before his engagement in Weimar. He had begun to develop it in 1895, as a result of his first teaching experience at the Université Libre of Brussels and the difficulty he faced in establishing his own artist's workshop, which was inspired by the British arts and crafts guilds, though without their stylistic preference for Neo-Gothic and their distrust of mechanical production. Originally trained as a painter, van de Velde soon commandeered other crafts: from graphic art, book design and dressmaking to interiors and architecture, he was always interested in form, material and technology. Bridging the distance between design and production and housing them under the same roof—he cleared the way for an innovative exploration of new artistic methods: there were early experiments with colored woodcut printing and later ones with metal ceramic glazes to generate color gradients for pottery, not to mention the display of steel trusses and concrete beams in his buildings. In addition, the experimental workshops have to be read as part of van de Velde's lifelong reformist thinking, inspired by Nietzsche's notion of authentic unity between art and life beyond academic knowledge (historism) and traditional learning (imitation), as envisioned in the second of the *Untimely Meditations: On the Use and Disadvantages of History for Life*.

From this historical trace, the Bauhaus also inherited theoretical conflicts such as the late romantic ideal of the synthesis of art versus industrial design, individual artistic expression versus rationalist efficiency or the opposing visions of the socialist guild society (the term "Bauhaus" recalling the medieval mason's lodge) and the research laboratory model as already imagined by van de Velde—unsolved questions of modernity that are still with us today.

BIBLIOGRAPHY
• Hellrag, Fritz. "Die grossherzogliche Kunstgewerbe-schule in Weimar." In *Kunstgewerbeblatt. Neue Folge*. V.22 No. 12, September 1911, 221–239.
• Nietzsche, Friedrich. *Unzeitgemässe Betrachtungen. Zweites Stück. Vom Nutzen und Nachtheil der Historie für das Leben*. Leipzig: Fritzsch, 1874.
• ——. *Untimely Mediations II: On the Uses and Disadvantages of History for Life*. Translated by R. J. Hollingdale, Cambridge/New York: Cambridge University Press, 1983; 1997.
• Sembach, Klaus-Jürgen. *Henry van de Velde*. New York: Rizzoli, 1989.

HENRY VAN DE VELDE *Ole W. Fischer*

1   Henry van de Velde, large amphora for Villa Esche, Chemnitz, executed by Reinhold Hanke, Höhr, in 1902; the violet-blue effects of the glaze result from experiments with metal pigments, to avoid the traditional toxic lead borosilicate. (Kunstsammlungen Chemnitz, Inv. Nr. II/115, height: 60 cm, stoneware, high-firing glaze, photo: May Voigt.

2   Portrait of Henry van de Velde in his studio at the "Kunstgewerbeschule Weimar" 1907, next to a theater study for Louise Dumont in Weimar, photo: Louis Held.

1

2

210

CODA

STRUCTURAL OSCILLATIONS
Installation for the 11th Venice Architecture Biennale
Swiss Pavilion, 2008

Gramazio & Kohler, Architecture and
Digital Fabrication, ETH Zurich

Michael Knauss (project leader)
Tobias Bonwetsch
Michael Lyrenmann
Ralph Bärtschi
Gregor Bieri
Michael Bühler
Hannes Oswald
Lukas Pauer

Partners:
Keller AG Ziegeleien
KUKA
Sika Schweiz AG

For the exhibition "Explorations," which addresses issues of design research and teaching in architecture, Gramazio & Kohler conceived a 100-meter-long brick wall to run as a continuous ribbon through the Swiss Pavilion. The wall installation was built on site at the Giardini, the grounds of the Biennale in Venice, by the R-O-B mobile robotic fabrication unit. With its looped form, the wall defines an involuted central space and an interstitial space beyond, between the brick wall and the existing structure of the pavilion. Passing from one space to the other, the visitor gains access to the exhibition. Through its materiality and spatial configuration, the wall, consisting of 14,961 individually rotated bricks, enters into a direct dialogue with the modernist brick structure from 1951 by Swiss architect Bruno Giacometti.

The wall's design was conceived as a system with open parameters. The course of a single, continuous curve carried all the generative information necessary to determine the design. This curve functioned as a conceptual interface, which enabled the needs of the individual exhibited groups to be negotiated. As each group's requirements were modified, the three-dimensional, undulating wall could be automatically regenerated. Its complex shape was determined by the constructive requirement that each single, four meter long segment should stand firmly on its own. Where the course of the generative curve was almost straight, meaning that the wall elements could possibly be tipped over by the visitors, the wall's footprint began to swing, thus increasing its stability. Each curvature in the lower layers was balanced by a counter-curvature in the upper layers, thus giving the wall its architectural expression. The wall loop adapted its shape according to its course, widening and narrowing, producing tension-rich spaces to lead visitors through the exhibition. In addition, the individual bricks were rotated according to the curvature—the greater the concavity of the curve, the more the bricks were rotated. This further emphasized the plastic malleability of the wall, which acquired an almost textile character, in oscillating contrast to the firm materiality of the bricks.

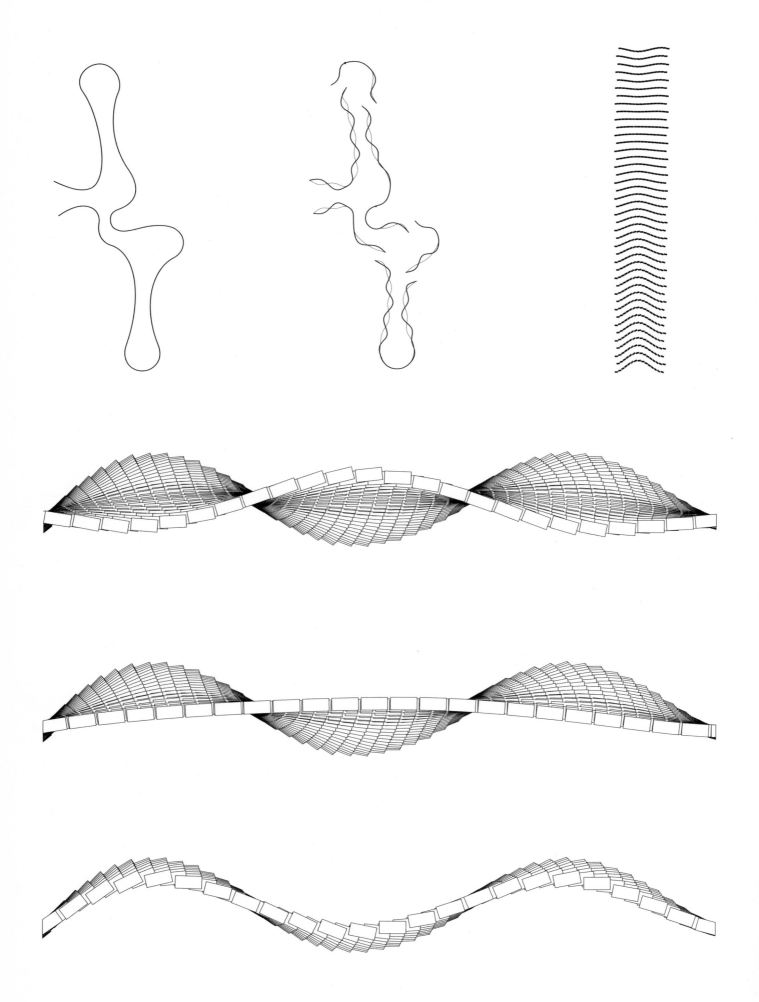

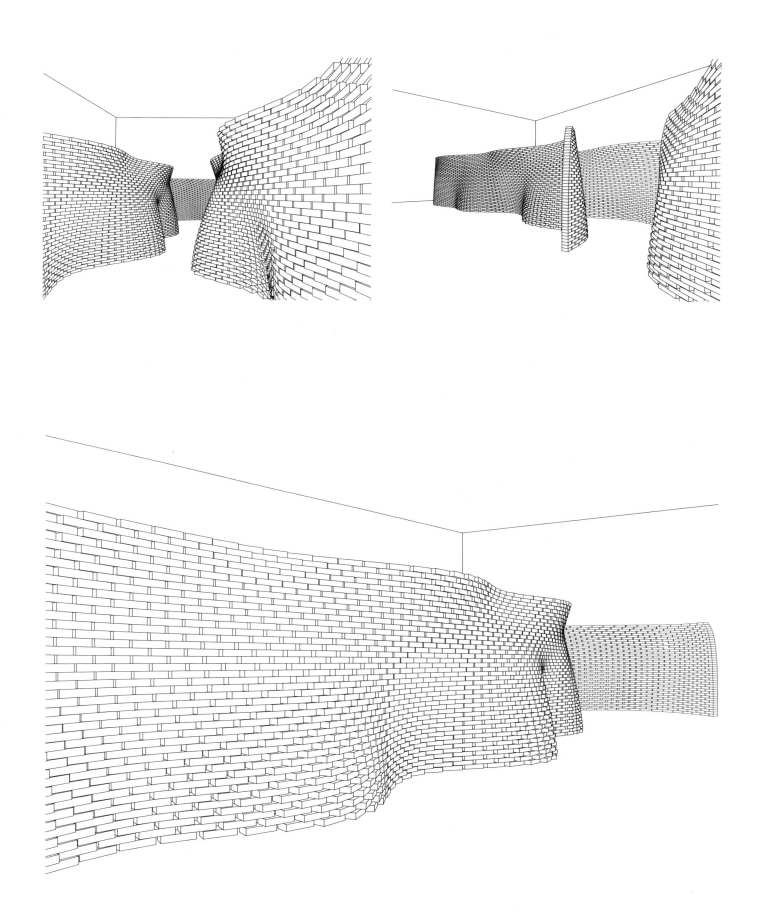

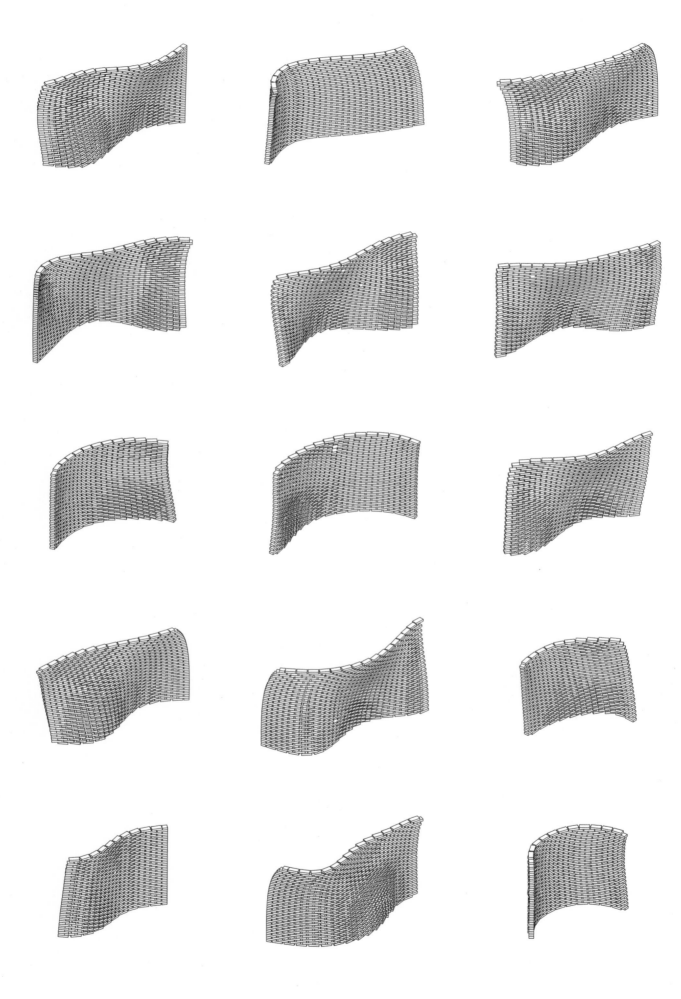

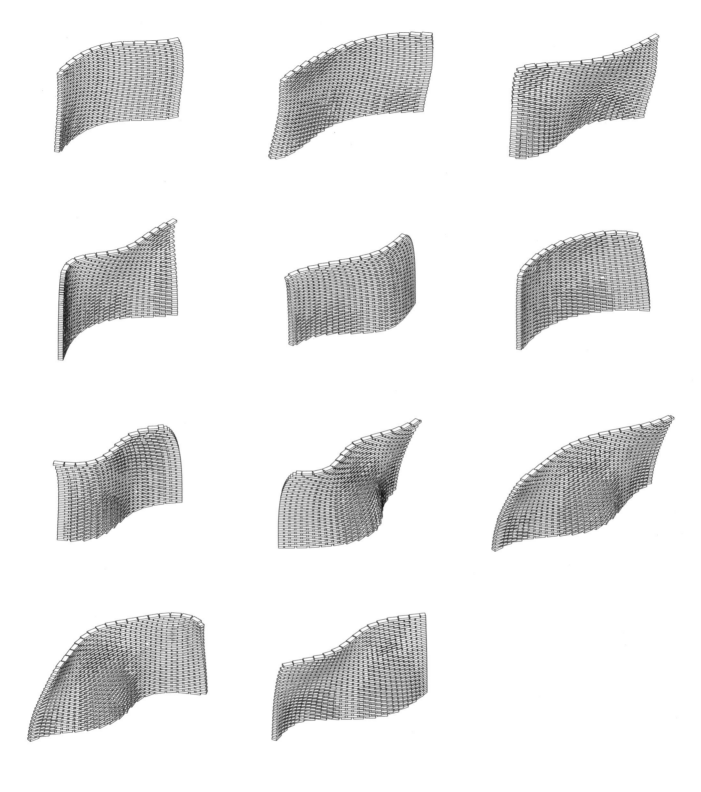

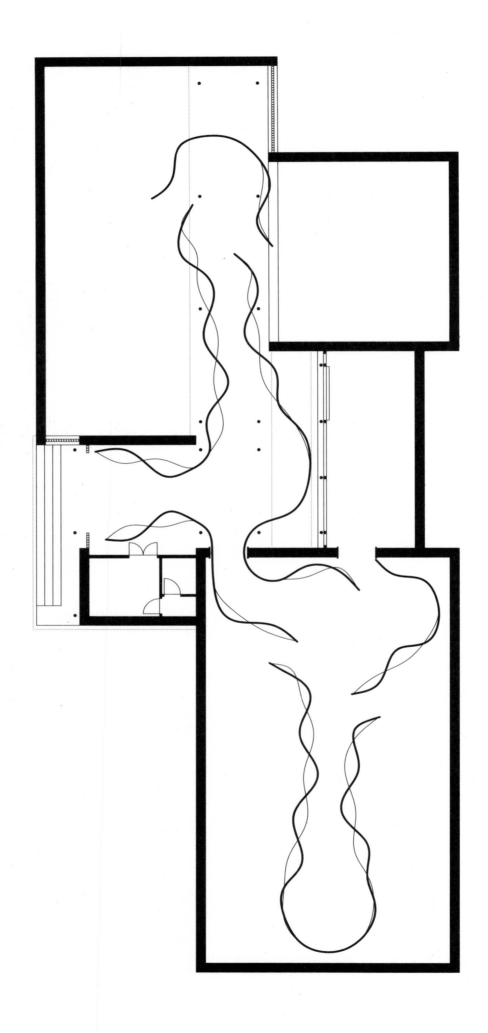